NeoVouchers

NeoVouchers
The Emergence of Tuition Tax Credits for Private Schooling

Kevin G. Welner

ROWMAN & LITTLEFIELD PUBLISHERS, INC.

Lanham • Boulder • New York • Toronto • Plymouth, UK

ROWMAN & LITTLEFIELD PUBLISHERS, INC.

Published in the United States of America
by Rowman & Littlefield Publishers, Inc.
A wholly owned subsidiary of The Rowman & Littlefield Publishing Group, Inc.
4501 Forbes Boulevard, Suite 200, Lanham, Maryland 20706
www.rowmanlittlefield.com

Estover Road, Plymouth PL6 7PY, United Kingdom

British Library Cataloguing in Publication Information Available

Library of Congress Cataloging-in-Publication Data

Welner, Kevin Grant, 1963–
  NeoVouchers : providing public funds for private schools through tuition tax credits /
Kevin G. Welner.
    p. cm.
  Includes bibliographical references and index.
  ISBN-13: 978-0-7425-4079-8 (cloth : alk. paper)
  ISBN-10: 0-7425-4079-0 (cloth : alk. paper)
  ISBN-13: 978-0-7425-4080-4 (pbk. : alk. paper)
  ISBN-10: 0-7425-4080-4 (pbk. : alk. paper)
  eISBN-13: 978-0-7425-6581-4
  eISBN-10: 0-7425-6581-5
  1. Educational vouchers—United States. 2. Tuition tax credits—United States. I. Title.
LB2828.8.W455 2008
379.1'110973—dc22

                                                                              2008026667

Printed in the United States of America

∞™ The paper used in this publication meets the minimum requirements of American
National Standard for Information Sciences—Permanence of Paper for Printed Library
Materials, ANSI/NISO Z39.48-1992.

Contents

Preface

MY INTEREST IN THIS SUBJECT was ignited when Arizona State University (ASU) professor Gene Glass asked me to participate in a symposium to be presented at the 2000 annual meeting of the American Educational Research Association. Arizona's Supreme Court had just upheld that state's tuition tax credit law, and Gene's colleague, Glen Wilson (then a doctoral candidate at ASU; currently a professor at the University of Northern Arizona), had begun researching the law's effects. Gene asked me to weigh in on the legal issues.[1]

A couple of years later, ASU professor Alex Molnar asked me to write two additional analyses of the Arizona law for his policy center, the Education Policy Research Unit. At about the same time, a bill proposing a law similar to Arizona's was introduced in my home state of Colorado, and it appeared to stand a solid chance of passage. I wrote an analysis of that bill for the Education and the Public Interest Center at the University of Colorado at Boulder. (The tax credit bill was eventually tabled in favor of a bill creating a direct voucher policy.)

As a result of such work, I thought more and more about this increasingly pervasive and important new policy (Pennsylvania and Florida had enacted similar tax credit laws in 2001) coupled with a dearth of scholarship. The disconnect seemed particularly stark given the enormous amount of extant research concerning direct voucher policies. It was as if all the music critics in 1970 were writing about the Kinks and ignoring the Beatles.

In general, my research focuses on the area of intersection between law and policy, thus placing these new tuition tax credit policies squarely in my court. And from the outset it was clear that the policies make for a fascinating case study for those of us interested in the intricacies of policy-making and constitutional nuance. They also implicate core issues concerning the public and the private in American schooling, how best to provide opportunities to the most disadvantaged American students, and the current American (and global) attraction to market-based social policies.

My progress in writing this book was helped immeasurably by the staff and leadership who make possible the Rockefeller Foundation's Bellagio Center residencies. I am grateful for their hospitality and am happy that this book will forever be entwined for me with my memories of interdisciplinary scholarship at their Italian villa. I am also ever grateful for the support of my colleagues at the University of Colorado at Boulder's School of Education and for the comments and feedback from Don Weitzman and Holly Yettick. Of course, the views and ideas presented in this book are those of the author and not necessarily those of anyone providing funding or assistance.

As someone who strongly values the public, societal role of schooling, I have attempted to approach the topic of tuition tax credit policies with an open mind to strengths as well as weaknesses. I have tried to understand and fairly present the reasoning underlying the policies and the justifications for their adoption, while never falling into the trap of feigned objectivity. Accordingly, it is my hope that this book is found to be useful and interesting by the staunchest opponents as well as the staunchest supporters of the voucher and tax credit policies—and even by some of those folks in between.

Note

1. The papers from that symposium from Glen Wilson, myself, Michele Moses, and Anthony Rud were published in *Education Policy Analysis Archives*.

1

Introduction

For most of the past half century, publicly supported schools shared some basic characteristics. Attendance was free, admission was (with some notable exceptions) open to all, instruction included little or no overt teaching of religion, and enrollment in a specific school was almost always based on the location of a child's residence. In recent years, school choice reforms such as open enrollment and charter schools have revolutionized this last element: parents in many jurisdictions may now choose from a variety of public schools, even schools far from their homes.

The other characteristics of publicly supported schools have largely remained intact, but now these too are changing. As illustrated by school voucher policies, each of these other characteristics is being reexamined. Such voucher policies seek to move the nation toward an educational system driven by market forces rather than by traditional democratic principles (Chubb and Moe, 1990). Yet vouchers still affect very few students.

In 2002, the U.S. Supreme Court upheld the federal constitutionality of Cleveland's voucher policy in the case of *Zelman v. Simmons-Harris*. At the time, Cleveland's plan was one of only three publicly funded voucher plans in the nation; Florida and Milwaukee rounded out the triumvirate. (As discussed in chapter 2, Maine and Vermont have similar policies, but the funding can only be used for non-religious schools.) Consistent with expectations among many observers, legislators around the nation responded to the *Zelman* decision by introducing voucher bills. Only in Arizona, Colorado, Louisiana, Ohio, Washington DC, Georgia, and Utah, however, did voucher bills of one form or another (often targeted to students in special education programs) become law. And even these laws did not necessarily survive. Two years after it passed, Colorado's law was declared unconstitutional, in violation of a local-control provision in that state's constitution (*Owens v. Colorado Congress of Parents*, 2004). Less than two years later, Florida's law was also found to violate its state constitution (*Bush v. Holmes*, 2006). Utah's ambitious voucher law was repealed by the state's voters—by a margin of 62 to 38 percent—before it even took effect (Gehrke, 2007). Most recently Arizona's legislature defunded its voucher laws (Kossan, 2008). Even Washington DC's voucher law is on the ropes (Turque, 2008).

While these voucher policies have struggled with expansion, the past decade has quietly seen a related policy transform education in three states and gain a foothold in three others. Tuition tax credit laws—kissing cousins of voucher systems—are now firmly entrenched in Arizona, Florida, and Pennsylvania, and they have recently been introduced in Georgia, Iowa, and Rhode Island. In addition, more students receive these voucher-like grants through such tuition tax credits than receive conventional vouchers. As presented in chapter 2, the voucher programs in Milwaukee and Cleveland may have garnered far greater media attention, but the tuition tax credit programs in Arizona and Pennsylvania are each larger than those two voucher programs combined. While vouchers have grabbed the headlines, tuition tax credits have grabbed the students.

Overview of This Book

Chapter 2 draws on the history of the voucher movement and the research that has grown out of that movement to ground and introduce the new tuition tax credit approach. Chapter 3 builds on that foundation, discussing the nature and history of tax incentive approaches to providing assistance for the education of students in such schools. It explains the key concept of "tax expenditures" and traces the evolution of tax policies, including the older form of tuition tax credit, which directly offsets parental educational expenses. Chapter 4 examines the existing research about the current tuition tax credit policies in Arizona, Florida, and Pennsylvania. This research begins to describe the inherent tradeoffs—an issue returned to in the book's final chapter.

Chapter 5 shifts focus to the legal issues surrounding vouchers in general and tuition tax credits in particular. Legal obstacles have always been a big part of the voucher story, and the same is true of tax credits. This chapter explores such legal challenges, focusing in particular on the possibility that the circuitous structure of tax credit laws may allow them to survive legal scrutiny even in states where voucher laws are found to be unconstitutional.

Chapter 6 then looks at the political and policy implications of the tuition tax credit approach, drawing comparisons to direct vouchers—noting advantages as well as concerns. For instance, the tax credit approach arguably has state budgetary advantages. But as compared to means-tested voucher plans, tuition tax credits tend to favor wealthier parents (those who owe substantial taxes).

Finally, chapter 7 begins with an explanation of why each law's details matter, examining some of the more important of those details: means-testing, public-school transfer requirements, the earmarking of donations, and whether the tax credit is for 100 percent of a donation. Based on what researchers have learned from existing policies, I offer a set of features that could be included in future legislation to help yield equitable outcomes. But even the recommended provisions would leave in place key drawbacks that policymakers should seriously consider before moving forward. These, too, are discussed. Moreover, the constitutional approach that favors tuition tax credits (as compared to vouchers) presents some difficult "slippery slope" issues. If tax credits are not considered government allocations, then what would realistically be left of the establishment clause? Could a similar mechanism not be used to pay the salaries of church ministers? Could that rationale not be used to allow positive check-offs on state and federal taxes to fund any religious institution or activity? After a discussion of such issues, the book concludes by relating tuition tax credits back to the broader choice discourse, discussing the democratic implications of these programs.

Conclusion

Perhaps the most important and widely accepted goal of the American educational system is the provision of high-quality educational opportunities to every student. Advocates of tuition tax credits and vouchers point out that the public school system has failed to accomplish this goal. They argue that system-changing privatization reforms hold the potential to broaden opportunities, particularly for at-risk children in low-income households.

As a means of providing equity and improving achievement for impoverished students currently enrolled in states' public education systems, however, tuition tax credit systems face daunting obstacles. This book offers a comprehensive exploration of the record and potential of tuition tax credit policies with regard to this goal and others. As compared to true voucher policies, tax credit policies are more pervasive and more likely to survive legal challenge. Yet these tuition tax credit policies—these neovouchers—have managed to fly under the voucher radar. A careful examination is overdue.

2

"Something So Close to Vouchers"

For more than fifty years, a dedicated group of free-market enthusiasts has promoted the idea of government-funded vouchers to help families pay for private schooling. And for the past two to three decades, this idea has been gaining traction among some equity-minded reformers seeking alternatives for students seeking to leave troubled inner-city schools. These groups have faced considerable obstacles—legal and political—as well as less-than-remarkable empirical results from pilot programs. All the while, the number of students receiving vouchers has continued a slow but steady ascendancy. This chapter draws on the history of the voucher movement and the research base that has grown out of that movement to shed light on the new tuition tax credit approach. As we shall see, the *raison d'être* of the new approach cannot be understood without first understanding the laws and politics of vouchers.

Raised in Arizona

Tuition tax credit policies fall into two broad categories. The older form directly offsets parental educational expenses including private school tuition.[1] For instance, a parent who incurs expenses for school books, tuition, or a child's computer may take a credit on state taxes to partially reimburse those expenses. These laws have existed in Minnesota and Iowa for decades, and Illinois adopted such a policy in 1999. Louisiana joined this group in 2008. As will be discussed in chapter 3, these types of individual tax credits, while important, do not imitate vouchers and, in comparison to their younger

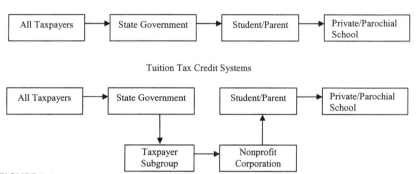

FIGURE 2.1
Comparison of Voucher and Tuition Tax Credit Systems

namesakes, have a more limited effect in reshaping the schooling landscape. They are not a major focus of this book.

In 1997, Arizona became the first state to adopt the second type of tuition tax credit policy, which I call *neovouchers*.[2] At that time, five years before the landmark *Zelman* case, Arizona legislators were unsure of the legality of voucher legislation under the U.S. Constitution. They turned to tuition tax credits as a non-traditional path toward the same goals. In a nutshell, the tax credit mechanism lets those who owe state taxes reallocate some of that money from the state general fund to a "scholarship-granting" organization (the legislation refers to the voucher-like grants as scholarships). In contrast to voucher plans, which deliver state-allocated funds to schools through the private decisions of parents, tax credit plans insert two intermediate steps into the process (see figure 2.1). First, the grants are issued by privately created, non-profit, scholarship-granting organizations, rather than directly by the government. Second, state allocation is achieved through a dollar-for-dollar tax credit given to donating taxpayers. Tuition tax credit systems are designed to provide government support for private schooling but to do so without any direct state payments. To accomplish this, tuition money passes through more hands before making its way to private and parochial schools, but the overall policy effect is very much the same as with vouchers (Hoxby and Murarka, 2006). Figure 2.1 describes the path taken by money under each of the two types of systems.

Effectively, this tax credit system still results in the government footing the tuition bill—through directly foregone revenues. For practical purposes, the state reimburses the taxpayer. But, as compared to voucher systems, control over funding decisions is largely delegated to two additional parties: (a) a subgroup of individual taxpayers, who can decide to which scholarship-granting

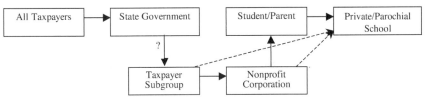

FIGURE 2.2
Further Look at Tuition Tax Credit Systems

organizations they will allocate the funds, and (b) the scholarship-granting organizations, which are given the authority to decide grant recipients. Such effective control is illustrated by a revised diagram showing the money's path (figure 2.2).

This added complexity, whereby a direct governmental expenditure is transformed into something more obscure, has been criticized as the public-sector version of money laundering (Associated Press, 2003). But the complexity serves important political and legal purposes. In particular, the question mark in figure 2.2 represents a key area of controversy: When the government provides a tax credit, is the taxpayer effectively receiving money from the government? If not, then constitutional restrictions placed on governmental activities and expenditures may not apply to tax credit policies. This issue is addressed in detail in chapter 5.

The dotted lines in figure 2.2 represent control that the person or organization may have over the money's destination. For instance, an Arizonian owing state taxes is given a series of choices. Most fundamentally, she can decide that she would rather have her money go to fund private schooling than go into the state's general fund. Beyond that, she can decide the nature of the private schooling that she will be supporting. She may, for instance, decide to donate her money to *Arizona Adventist Scholarships, Inc.,* a so-called school tuition organization (STO) created by or on behalf of private Seventh-day Adventist schools. In theory, this STO could give scholarships to families planning to attend Catholic or secular private schools, but this is unlikely given the organization's mission. While it is true that the Arizona law requires all STOs to be associated with at least two schools (see chapter 4), the mere association does not guarantee that the vouchers will be split between the two or more schools. In fact, some STOs have steered all vouchers to a single school (Arizona Department of Revenue, 2006). For this reason and others, the STO and, in effect, the taxpayer can target the money with a great deal of specificity.

As noted above, Arizona legislators turned to this tax credit system as a legally cautious way to achieve voucher goals. Backers of this policy intended it to mirror vouchers in basic approach and effect. They were not disappointed.

The free-market Milton and Rose Friedman Foundation ranked Arizona's tax credit program a close second (to Florida's McKay Scholarships) as the nation's top school choice program (Enlow, 2004, 9–10). Consider also the statement of John Huppenthal, then-chair of the Arizona Senate's Education Committee, who had been a longtime voucher supporter: "This has turned into something so close to vouchers you almost can't tell the difference" (Bland, 2000, A22). Or, as rhetorically asked by Trent Franks, the former Arizona legislator and activist credited with originating the tax credit idea, "Why do we need vouchers at this point?" (Bland, 2000, A22).

Tax Credit and Voucher Policy Rationales

Even for those who are not enthusiastic backers of market-based educational policies, the basic appeal of voucher or tax credit legislation is understandable. Nationally, children in low-income families attend public schools with the least experienced and least trained teachers, with the most school overcrowding, with the worst facilities, and generally with the least challenging classes (Darling-Hammond et al., 1996; Darling-Hammond, 2000; NCTAF, 2004; Ravitch, 2001; Ready, Lee, and Welner, 2004; Oakes, 1985, 2005). These families are therefore the most in need of schooling alternatives, yet they can least afford to choose the option of nonpublic schools. "Means-tested" voucher and tax credit systems—that is, those systems that tie eligibility to a showing of financial need—promise to provide some immediate relief to these students and their parents (Howe, 1997).

Applying this rationale, voucher advocates immediately cast the Supreme Court's decision in *Zelman* (2002) as a civil rights victory on par with *Brown v. Board of Education* (1954). Vouchers, the argument goes, advance equity because they place poor (often minority) students on a more equal playing field with students from wealthier families, who have always had more extensive options in choosing their neighborhoods and schools (Coons and Sugarman, 1978; Viteritti, 1999). President Bush, in a speech in Cleveland delivered soon after the *Zelman* ruling was handed down, praised it as "just as historic" as *Brown* (Bush, 2002). Education Secretary Rod Paige wrote an opinion piece in which he concluded, "With *Brown*, education became a civil rights issue, and the decision introduced a civil rights revolution that continues to this day. *Zelman v. Simmons-Harris* holds the same potential. It recasts the education debates in this country, encouraging a new civil rights revolution and ushering in a 'new birth of freedom' for parents and their children everywhere in America" (Paige, 2002).

In keeping with this civil rights language, voucher advocates have, to date, largely focused their rhetoric and efforts on these at-risk children—forming and funding groups like the Black Alliance for Educational Options and including means-testing in private and public voucher systems (Gill et al., 2007; People for the American Way, 2003, Appendix A). Tuition tax credit laws, too, have been advanced as an equity-minded policy, designed to help low-income families with at-risk children opt for private schooling. Florida's tax credit is means-tested, as are Pennsylvania's, Iowa's, and Rhode Island's—though the latter three feature substantially higher income limits. Moreover, even though the tax credit laws in Arizona and Georgia include no means-testing provision, backers promoted them as primarily benefiting the poor (Keegan, 2001; McCutchen, 2008).

Kelly McCutchen, executive vice president of the Georgia Public Policy Foundation, a main force behind that state's law, wrote that "flexibility in the law provides for full tuition scholarships to low-income students while middle-income students could be asked to pay a portion of the tuition" (McCutchen, 2008). But in fact the Georgia law is not means-tested; there are no requirements or incentives targeting the money to lower-income families. The law may technically "allow" for equitable outcomes, but it does little or nothing to pursue that goal.

The Arizona Supreme Court, in upholding that state's neovoucher law against a legal challenge, also stressed the potential benefits for low-income residents:

> [U]ntil now low-income parents may have been coerced into accepting public education. These citizens have had few choices and little control over the nature and quality of their children's schooling because they have been unable to afford a private education that may be more compatible with their own values and beliefs. Arizona's tax credit achieves a higher degree of parity by making private schools more accessible and providing alternatives to public education. (*Kotterman v. Killian*, 1999, 615)

Yet, notwithstanding this rhetorical use of poor families in passing and defending the law, the scholarships awarded through the Arizona tuition tax credit program appear to have provided relatively few actual benefits to these low-income parents (Bland, 2000; Wilson, 2002). In fact, one of the primary promoters for Arizona's tax credit policy has acknowledged the strategic use of low-income families, first admitting that the present system "probably" helps the middle class and wealthy more than the poor and then characterizing advocates' attempts to sell the program as helping poor children as "only an angle" (Kossan, 2002).

Of course, diverse supporters of vouchers and tax credits have based their support on a variety of different beliefs and goals. Some—like Polly Williams, a primary author of Wisconsin's voucher law—looked to the policy solely as a means of assisting low-income families (Molnar, 1997). Colorado's short-lived voucher law stressed, in its "legislative declaration" section, the challenge of "closing the achievement gap between high-performing and low-performing children, including the gap between minority and non-minority students and between economically disadvantaged students and their more advantaged peers" (Colo.Rev.Stat. 22-56-102(b)). In contrast, other voucher and tax credit advocates see means-tested policies merely as an important first step along a path to broader-based privatization reforms (Kossan, 2002). For members of this latter group, privatization and competition hold the potential to generate extensive improvements in the American educational system, shifting reliance from a moribund educational bureaucracy to a vibrant marketplace (Chubb and Moe, 1990; Friedman, 1962).

Voucher Programs

The modern era of publicly funded voucher policies began in the 1990s, when Wisconsin and Ohio adopted such policies for their largest and most troubled school districts—Milwaukee and Cleveland, respectively.[3] Milwaukee has the oldest and largest such program in the United States. This means-tested policy started in 1990 with a cap set at 1 percent of the district's enrollment. Legislation in 1995 increased the cap to 15 percent and also permitted religious schools to participate. Over time the program has expanded significantly. In 1997–98, 1,545 students received vouchers; in 1998–99, this number increased to 6,085. For the 2007–08 school year, the program enrollment topped 18,550 (Enlow, 2008; United States Department of Education, 2007).

Cleveland hosts the other well-established, publicly funded, means-tested voucher program active in the United States. The program has seen a gradual expansion from 1996–97 (1,994 recipients, grades K-3) to 2007–08 (6,195 recipients, grades K-12) (Enlow, 2008; United States Department of Education, 2007).

Florida's A+ voucher program, also called the Opportunity Scholarships Program, began in 1999 and continued until 2006, when it was found to violate the state constitution (*Bush v. Holmes*, 2006; see also chapter 5). It was not means-tested but did focus on students from low-performing schools, who are likely to be low income. Voucher eligibility was tied to the state's school-accountability system, based on the Florida Comprehensive Assessment Test (FCAT). If a school was deemed failing for any two years during a four-year period, its students would become eligible to receive an A+ voucher (Florida Department of Education, 2007c).

Florida also has two other voucher-like programs—both of which serve more students than did the A+ program, which provided only 734 vouchers in 2005–06 (United States Department of Education, 2007). The McKay Scholarship program, aimed at special education students, provided 18,919 students with vouchers in 2007–08 (Enlow, 2008; see also United States Department of Education, 2007). The tuition tax credit system, under which corporations fund neovouchers by donating money to the program and getting a dollar-for-dollar credit on their state taxes, funded 19,416 students in 2007–08 (Enlow, 2008; see also United States Department of Education, 2007).[4]

In addition to these established programs, Washington DC, Louisiana, and Ohio (among others) recently adopted voucher policies.[5] Table 2.1 offers some basic comparisons between these voucher programs in Milwaukee, Cleveland, Florida, Washington DC, Ohio, and New Orleans.

Tuition Tax Credit Programs

The tuition tax credit laws in Arizona, Florida, and Pennsylvania, as well as the new laws in Georgia, Iowa, and Rhode Island, differ in key respects. Until 2006, the most notable difference between the three older laws was that Arizona's program applied only to individual taxpayers, not corporations; in contrast, the laws in the other two states apply only to corporations, not individuals. Arizona's policy was, however, expanded in 2005 to include a corporate component. The three new states split in their chosen approach: Georgia provides a tax credit for both corporate and individual donations, Iowa provides a tax credit for only individual donations, and Rhode Island provides the credit for only corporations.

Another difference between the state laws concerns the overall annual amount of the tax credits. Arizona places no ceiling on the total amount of tax credits available each year for the individual taxpayer part of its policy, while in Florida the total amount of tax credits cannot exceed $118 million per fiscal year and in Pennsylvania the annual ceiling is $26.7 million (working essentially on a first-come-first-served basis). Arizona's new corporate tax credit began with a ceiling of $5 million per year, but that amount has been raised to $10 million in 2007 and increases annually thereafter by 20 percent. Georgia's law has an aggregate ceiling of $50 million, Iowa's ceiling was $2.5 million in 2006–07 and $7.5 million in 2008, and Rhode Island has by far the lowest ceiling: $1 million.

TABLE 2.1
Comparison of Publicly Funded Voucher Programs

Participating District or State	Year Begun	Eligibility Criteria	Number of Participating Students	Amount of Voucher
Milwaukee	1990	Family income up to 175% of poverty line.	18,550 students received vouchers in 2007–08, attending 122 different private schools.	Up to $6,501 or the private school's tuition.
Cleveland	1995	Family income up to 200% of poverty line, with priority for poorest.	6,195 students received vouchers in 2007–08, attending 45 different private schools.	The lesser of 90% of a private school's tuition or $3,450 (higher for special-needs students).
Florida*	1999	Students in attendance areas of public schools deemed failing for two years in a four-year period.	734 students received vouchers in 2005–06, attending 57 different private schools.	Average voucher amount was $4,205 in 2005–06.
Washington DC	2004	Family income up to 185% of poverty line.	1,800 students received vouchers in 2007–08, attending 68 different private schools.	Up to $7,500, not to exceed the school's normal tuition and other costs.
Ohio	2006	Students in attendance areas of public schools deemed failing for two years in a three-year period.	6,836 students received vouchers in 2007–08, attending 323 different private schools.	Up to $4,250 for elementary school and $5,000 for high school.
New Orleans	2008	Family income up to 250% of poverty line.	Approximately 200 students will receive vouchers in the program's first year.	The lesser of the private school's tuition or $6,300.

Source: Barrow (2008); Enlow (2008); United States Department of Education (2007).
* This table reports only the A+ voucher plan (it does not include the McKay Scholarships for special education students). However, Florida's A+ law has been found by the Florida Supreme Court to be in violation of the state constitution because it impaired the state's ability to provide a single system of free public schools (*Bush v. Holmes*, 2006).

Arizona provides a 100 percent tax credit for donations up to $1,000 per taxpaying couple. Corporations are now eligible for a similar 100 percent credit, with no cap on a donation. Florida's law also provides a dollar-for-dollar credit, with few meaningful limits on donations.[6] In Pennsylvania, however, the credit starts at 75 percent, increasing to 90 percent with a two-year commitment by the donor, and the credit per year for any given corporation may not exceed $200,000. Similar to Pennsylvania, Rhode Island gives corporations a 75 percent credit, or 90 percent if the second-year donation is worth at least 80 percent of the first year's donation, with a maximum credit per corporation of $100,000. Iowa offers a credit for individual taxpayers equal to 65 percent of the value of the contribution; there is no cap on the amount of a donation. Georgia's new law most closely resembles Arizona's in this regard, providing a 100 percent tax credit for both corporate and individual taxpayers.

The three established neovoucher programs account for more "vouchers" than do the traditional voucher programs (table 2.2). Combined, the three programs issued more than 90,500 voucher-like grants in 2007–08. In comparison, the voucher programs in Cleveland, Milwaukee, Washington DC, and Ohio distributed 33,400 vouchers. Adding in Florida's large McKay Scholarship program for special education students, the total increases to approximately 52,300—still less than 58 percent of the tax credit level. Moreover, the recent emergence of neovoucher policies—in Georgia, Iowa, and Rhode Island, as well as Arizona's corporate credit—substantially outpaces the additional voucher policies, largely limited to targeted, special education policies in Georgia, Ohio, and Utah. Accordingly, we can expect the numerical disparities to continue to grow.

TABLE 2.2
Numbers of Voucher and Tuition Tax Credit Recipients

	Vouchers		Tuition Tax Credits
State/District	*Number of Recipients (2007–08)*	*State*	*Number of Recipients (2007–08)*
Milwaukee	18,550	Arizona	27,153*
Cleveland	6,195	Florida	19,416
Florida (McKay)	18,919	Pennsylvania	44,000
Washington DC	1,800		
Ohio	6,836		
Total	**52,300**	**Total**	**90,569**

Source: Enlow (2008); United States Department of Education (2007).
*The Arizona data are only for the individual tax credit (corporate tax credit information is not included).

The tax credit laws in Arizona, Pennsylvania, and Florida include provisions designed to provide at least a nominal benefit to public as well as nonpublic schools. Arizona concurrently created a tax credit for donations to public schools, to support extracurricular activities (A.R.S. § 43-1089.01). If fully funded, approximately one-third of the Pennsylvania donations would go toward funding innovative educational programs for public school students. (That is, the cap for the private school program is approximately $26.7 million; the cap for the public school program is approximately $13.3 million.) Florida's law allows donated money to be used to subsidize transportation to an out-of-district public school. Georgia, Iowa, and Rhode Island do not include parallel provisions designed to assist public schools. The specifics of the laws in these six states are discussed in greater detail in chapter 4.

Voucher Research

Also as discussed in chapter 4, very few studies have been conducted on the effects of tuition tax credit programs. However, vouchers are an older policy and have now been the subject of some careful and comprehensive research that sheds light on the future prospects for, and the likely effects of, tax credits.

The voucher research itself is hardly conclusive, and, as William Howell has pointed out, "In their sheer volume, reviews of the small body of empirical work on school vouchers are beginning to eclipse the research literature itself" (Howell, 2002, p. 79). Existing voucher research has been reviewed by Martin Carnoy (2002), Patrick McEwan (2004), Brian Gill and his colleagues at Rand (2007), Helen Ladd (2003), and the U.S. General Accounting Office (2001, 2002).[7] In addition, research in this field has been advanced by various re-analyses of data (see, e.g., Greene, Peterson, and Du, 1996; Krueger and Zhu, 2004; Rouse, 1998).

The primary research in this field has been conducted, to a great extent, by three groups of researchers. Paul Peterson's group has been the most prolific, focusing its efforts on the three largest privately funded voucher plans, those of Dayton, Ohio; Washington DC; and New York City. Peterson's colleagues in these efforts have included William Howell, Jay P. Greene, Patrick Wolf, and Martin West.[8] In New York, Peterson's work was conducted in cooperation with Mathematica Policy Research.[9] For the most part, the original publication of this research was not peer reviewed, but the researchers have occasionally summarized that work in peer-reviewed articles (Howell, Wolf, Campbell, and Peterson, 2002; see also Wolf and Hoople, 2006). Most recently, Patrick Wolf has been the principal investigator of the publicly funded voucher program in Washington DC (Wolf et al., 2007, 2008).

Primary research for the two largest public school voucher plans, in Milwaukee and Cleveland, was conducted by contract researchers. Wisconsin contracted with political scientist John Witte to evaluate the Milwaukee plan; Ohio contracted with education researcher Kim Metcalfe to evaluate the Cleveland plan.[10] Peterson's group has conducted extensive secondary analyses of both programs.[11]

Effects on Voucher Recipients

The research on vouchers in the United States shows that parents who received vouchers are happy with their increased freedom and with the choices they have made. But on the key question of academic performance, the research only hints at small, isolated (non-robust) benefits. As Howell (2002) concluded, "On one issue there is general agreement: parents who use vouchers are more satisfied with their private schools than are parents who apply to voucher programs but remain in public schools. Everywhere else, however, the reviews turn up inconsistencies and disagreements."

In Cleveland and Milwaukee, studies have shown neither harm nor substantial benefit associated with the voucher policies. The state-funded evaluations yielded little that compellingly separates the achievement of voucher students from public school students. Re-analysis by Peterson and his colleagues disagreed, concluding that the data did show some isolated benefits associated with being a voucher student. Princeton economist Cecilia Rouse also found a benefit—in mathematics tests for Milwaukee voucher students (Rouse, 1998). In particular, she found that voucher students had, for mathematics, a 1.5 to 2.3 percentile point gain over their peers for each year spent in a private school. Yet she found no statistically significant increase in reading scores for the voucher students. Rouse (1998, 2000) has also argued that the positive effect for math is potentially due to smaller class sizes in the private schools.[12] (The robustness issues thus include the question of why smaller class size would not also raise reading scores.)

Early results from the publicly funded program in Washington DC similarly show no statistically significant achievement differences between voucher recipients and a control group in DC's public schools (Wolf et al., 2008). The study uses a random-assignment design, taking advantage of the district's lottery process. The overall findings offered nothing to support the hope that vouchers will improve students' academic achievement. Moreover, Congress's five-year funding allocation for the program expires after 2008, and all indications are that the new Congress will phase the program out beginning in 2008–2009 or the following year (Strauss and Turque, 2008; Turque, 2008).

Looking only at the older publicly funded voucher programs, the federal General Accounting Office noted that the contract research teams for Cleveland and Milwaukee (that is, the research led by Metcalf and by Witte) "found little or no statistically significant differences in voucher students' achievement test scores compared to public school students" (GAO, 2001, 27). But the GAO also mentioned that "other investigators found that voucher students did better in some subject areas tested," concluding that none of the findings could be "considered definitive because the researchers obtained different results when they used different methods to compensate for weaknesses in the data" (GAO, 2001, 27).

This pattern is illustrated by the turmoil surrounding the most positive and noteworthy findings to come from the Peterson group's research on privately funded programs. These researchers found statistically significant academic benefits associated with vouchers for African American students in the New York City program. The benefits were concentrated among African Americans who switched to private schools when they were entering the fifth grade, but these gains were large enough to produce a significant average gain for the entire New York sample of African Americans. No statistically significant academic benefits were apparent for the Dayton program studied by the same researchers. The Washington DC program, also studied by this research group, offered a hint of such benefits for African Americans, only to have these benefits disappear after the second year. No statistically significant academic benefits were found for Hispanic students in any of the three programs. Yet, although the positive results were limited, they nevertheless provided some evidence that vouchers may assist some low-income students of color (Gill et al., 2007; GAO, 2002).

The New York study turned out to be particularly controversial because the researchers at Mathematica Policy Research, who worked in cooperation with Peterson, almost immediately cautioned against the conclusion that vouchers increased student achievement (see Mathematica, 2003; Winerip, 2003). Subsequently, a reanalysis by two Princeton economists concluded that the significant benefits were not robust. Krueger and Zhu (2003) reinserted into the analysis students with missing baseline scores (thereby increasing the original sample by 44 percent) and expanded the definition of "African American" to include children with an African American father as well as those with an African American mother.[13] These two changes in the treatment of data eliminated the significant effects.[14] The upshot of all these analyses, taken together, is that the New York program may have yielded some benefit for some African American students. But the evidence from New York, as well as Dayton and Washington DC, also demonstrates that the voucher programs are generally not associated with any significant change in achievement.

More recently, several researchers have used large data sets to compare student achievement in private versus public schools. These associational studies have tended to show public school results that are at least as positive as results from private schools. Wenglinsky (2007) compared public and private schools in terms of students' learning outcomes as measured by standardized tests, using National Education Longitudinal Study (NELS) data concerning disadvantaged students in urban settings. Once key family background characteristics such as socioeconomic status and behaviors such as parental involvement were taken into account, he found attendance at private high schools was not associated with immediate academic advantages or longer-term advantages in attending college, finding satisfaction in the job market, or participating in civic life.

Similarly, analyses of National Assessment of Educational Progress (NAEP) mathematics data by Lubienski and Lubienski (2006a) and of NAEP math and reading data by Braun, Jenkins, and Grigg (2006) used hierarchical linear modeling to compare the academic achievement of private and public school students, controlling for demographic characteristics and school location. Both studies, using slightly different models, concluded that while the private school students had relatively high raw scores, those scores were accounted for by demographic differences. After controlling for these differences, public school students generally scored better than their private school peers in math and were equal in fourth-grade reading (the one instance of private schools retaining their advantage was for eighth-grade reading). These findings lend support for those who challenge the underlying achievement assumption of vouchers—that private schools will offer a higher-quality alternative for students seeking to leave public schools. In response, Paul Peterson has been highly critical of this NAEP research, arguing that the researchers specified the wrong models (Peterson and Llaudet, 2006).[15] But Lubienski and Lubienski (2008) recently published another study, using the Early Childhood Longitudinal Study, Kindergarten Class of 1998–99 (or ECLS-K) database to examine math scores of students in K through 5, and they again found that students in public schools perform at least as well as similar students in private schools (Lubienski and Lubienski, 2008).

As with the above-discussed research about academic consequences of vouchers, any overall conclusion fairly drawn from the "public versus private" research should be stated with caution. One cannot conclude from this associational research that private schools do not result in an academic benefit. Similarly, one cannot conclude that public schools do not result in an academic benefit. And one certainly cannot dismiss a claim that a given private or public school is beneficial. But a fair conclusion is that no substantial academic benefit is evident, on average, between sectors. Similarly, as things now stand, the complete body of voucher research fails to support claims that vouchers significantly boost student achievement.

Competition Effects on Public Schools

Advocates of vouchers often assert a need for competition to the public schooling system, which they describe as bureaucratic and moribund (Chubb and Moe, 1990; Friedman, 1962). Without competition, they argue, these schools have insufficient incentive to be efficient or to be excellent. In recent years, they have pointed to the research of Caroline Hoxby and Jay P. Greene as providing empirical support for the proposition that increased competition will drive public school improvement. The argument here is that vouchers benefit even those in public schools who never actually receive a voucher, and some studies have indeed found evidence of an association between greater competition and higher student achievement (see discussion in Belfield and Levin, 2002).

Hoxby (2002, 2003a, 2003b) has studied school competition in various forms, including charter schools and vouchers. Focusing on charter schools in Arizona and Michigan and the voucher program in Milwaukee, she concluded that the productivity of public schools increased when exposed to competition. The design for her study of Milwaukee's program involved a comparison between fourth-grade achievement in three groups of schools: those that faced the greatest voucher threat (those with the most low-income, eligible students), those with an intermediate level of voucher threat, and those with no voucher threat. She found that schools in the first group had the most growth in achievement, an effect she attributed to competition. One critique of this work has been offered by Ladd (2003), who points to the straightforward effect of removing lower-scoring students from a public school.[16]

Greene (2001) makes an argument similar to Hoxby's using data from Florida's now-terminated A+ voucher program (see also Greene and Winters, 2003; West and Peterson, 2006), as well as from the McKay Scholarship voucher program (Greene and Winters, 2008). The A+ program was very limited, targeted only at students who attended schools receiving the state's lowest rating. These schools were required to improve or face the prospect that their students would be offered vouchers to attend other schools (public or private). Greene concluded that students in these schools improved at a greater rate than those without the so-called voucher threat. That is, the educators at these schools found ways to improve, in order to avoid the sanction of having the state give vouchers to the schools' students.

However, Greene's study was heavily criticized (see Camilli and Bulkley, 2001; Carnoy, 2002; and Kupermintz, 2001). The main criticisms have focused on three issues. First, the study failed to adequately account for a statistical phenomenon called regression to the mean. Second, although the study attributes school improvement to the threat of vouchers, Florida policy also included other incentives, disincentives, and assistance aimed at these poorly performing schools. Third, Kupermintz (2001) in particular emphasized the specific way that many failing schools were able to improve their scores. For example, they taught their students some simple and relatively superficial ways to pass the writing test.[17] Consistent with the second point, Figlio and Rouse (2006) offered evidence suggesting that the Florida gains were in fact primarily due to the stigma of being labeled a low-achieving school rather than the threat of vouchers.

A more recent study by Greene and Winters (2003) reached the same conclusions as their study two years earlier, but the authors expressly addressed areas of criticism from their earlier paper, concluding that the explanations offered as alternatives to the "voucher threat" can be safely ruled out. This second study engendered much less press attention and critical reaction than the earlier one.[18] Moreover, a recent working paper by Cecilia Rouse and her colleagues also found that among the school-level responses associated with the A+ program were educational improvements and associated positive outcomes (Rouse, Hannaway, Goldhaber, and Figlio, 2007).

Most recently, Greene and Winters (2008) analyzed Florida's McKay Scholarship program for students with special needs, again finding that competition had a beneficial effect on nearby public schools. A review of that work, however, found research design problems, failure to take into account alternative explanations, and unsubstantiated assumptions about the direction of possible selection bias (Yun, 2008).

American Enterprise Institute scholar Rick Hess (2002) also argued that vouchers can have a positive competitive effect. However, based on his review of the research and his own studies of Cleveland, Milwaukee, and a privately funded voucher program in San Antonio, he concluded that this effect is not yet substantial. He explained that, instead of responding to the increased competition by improving quality or efficiency, public school policymakers and educators tend to focus their energies on "mobilizing popular sentiment or on taking marginal actions that will allay the concerns of vocal constituencies" (Hess, 2002, 52; see also Teske, Schneider, Buckley, and Clark, 2000).

As Hess suggests, competitive responses are not confined to improved quality or efficiency (see Lubienski, 2005). Paul Hill noted that competition resulting from the expansion of charter schools is often merely cosmetic: "Even in places where charters serve a significant segment of the public school market, districts have done little more than adjust marketing strategies to compete" (Hill, 2007, 27). And some research has shown detrimental competition effects in terms of achievement at nearby public schools (Carr and Ritter, 2007). Most troubling, perhaps, are incentives that might discourage schools from serving the neediest populations. Lubienski and Gulosino (2007) used GIS mapping to analyze charter school location decisions in Detroit; their analysis suggests that competitive pressures may lead to a sorting of clients, with segments of the charter school sector gravitating toward desirable clients and minimizing risk by avoiding others. While they found some charter schools to be serving at-risk and minority populations, they also found that these schools were disproportionately "mission-oriented" charters. Profit-oriented charters—the schools most responsive to market incentives—avoided these neighborhoods.

Consistent with these findings, the research on choice behavior suggests that families choose schools based more on demographics than on direct evidence of academic quality (Lacireno-Paquet and Brantley, 2008). White parents tend to avoid schools with high minority concentrations; minority parents tend to opt for schools with lower percentages of low-income students. Moreover, although formal information provided by schools and the state can be useful, most parents appear to rely more heavily on information and suggestions from networks of friends, colleagues, and others (Teske and Reichardt, 2006). These studies about choice behavior suggest that increased competition may facilitate greater parental engagement in response to incentives, but that these incentives will often focus on school features other than academic quality.

Macro-policy Effects on At-risk Students in Low-income Families

In addition to the possible advantages argued by Greene, Peterson, Hoxby, and others, vouchers and other forms of choice may have a negative effect on low-income families, due to harms suffered by the public schools that these students generally attend (Nelson et al., 2001). These claims generally focus on fiscal issues. If state funding is diverted to tuition and other costs of private schooling, then less money may be left for public schools.

Importantly, this will not always be the case—each state's funding policies and specific voucher policy will result in different fiscal effects on public schools. The Utah voucher law that existed for a short time in 2007, for instance, included so-called hold harmless provisions, whereby a public school would continue to receive the difference between the cost of the voucher and the average funding per student for a pupil who leaves that school using a voucher. But this sort of hold-harmless provision is unusual. In fact, some of the staunchest supporters of vouchers see fiscal squeeze as an important element of competition and long-term improvement of public schools.

Another counter-argument voiced by voucher supporters looks beyond the direct effects of vouchers on individual public schools and focuses more broadly on overall fiscal impact. Vouchers often have a face value that is less than the full cost students would impose on the state if they were still in public schools. If, for example, a year of public schooling costs $6,000, and the voucher is for only $3,000, then the state saves $3,000 every time a student uses a voucher to transfer from public to private school. Accordingly, the overall fiscal effect of a voucher policy will depend on a variety of factors, including the following: (a) whether the policy includes any sort of funding guarantee for public schools, (b) whether students currently attending private schools are eligible to receive the vouchers, and (c) the dollar amount attached to each voucher.

Another concern of public school advocates is that the response described by Hess (2002) will lead to inefficiencies. That is, "mobilizing popular sentiment" in favor of a given public school does not help to educate public school students. Instead, it diverts the time, energy, and money of educators away from their primary task.

Even if one assumes that a voucher or tax credit plan would yield a better education for participating students, important policy questions remain concerning the move away from public education. Is it proper for the state to accomplish its educational goals through a policy that requires low-income parents to pay a substantial portion of the education's cost? Why would a state want to move poor families from a system that covers the entire cost of their education into one where only a fraction is covered? In public schools, families are not asked to pay tuition, and students cannot be turned away because they are too poor, too disabled, or of the wrong religion. Before seriously considering this policy option, must the state have already concluded that it cannot realistically provide a quality education to all children through the free public school system? These questions raise important issues to be considered by any policymaker considering tuition tax credit legislation.

Finally, as discussed in the next section of this chapter, the strength of a public school is often due to the families it serves; loss of efficacious families is another drain on public school resources.

Stratification and Skimming

Research into school choice programs has documented troubling patterns of segregation by income, race, achievement level, English-language learners, and special education status (Arsen et al., 2000; Cobb and Glass, 1999; Cullen, Jacob, and Levitt, 2005, 2006; Fiske and Ladd, 2000; Frankenberg and

Lee, 2003; Howe, Eisenhart and Betebenner, 2001; Howe and Welner, 2002; Hsieh and Urquiola, 2003; Rothstein, 1999). An early and still influential study was conducted by Cobb and Glass (1999), looking at Arizona charter school enrollment. It compared racial patterns of enrollment in charter schools with the enrollment in their neighboring public schools, finding that the charter schools had a significantly higher proportion of white students. A case study of a choice-intensive school district in Colorado also found racial stratification patterns (Howe, Eisenhart, and Betebenner, 2001). Research into New Zealand's universal school choice plan similarly showed substantial stratification (Fiske and Ladd, 2000), as has research into the comprehensive voucher program in Chile (Hsieh and Urquiola, 2002)—although the stratification in these overseas studies was by characteristics other than race.

Using a household-level data set for eight metropolitan areas in upstate New York, Lankford and Wyckoff (2005) analyzed the relative role played by a variety of factors, including race, in modeling choices between public and private schooling options. They found that race has a direct and an indirect (through correlates to race, such as parental education) effect on choice-based racial stratification. They also confirmed the finding from other studies that white families are less likely to choose schools having higher percentages of minority students (see Lankford and Wyckoff, 2005, 22, and studies cited therein).

Weiher and Tedin (2002) analyzed charter school households in Texas and found that whites, African Americans, and Hispanics all tended to transfer to schools with higher levels of students of the same race/ethnicity. And Miron and Nelson (2002) examined the composition of individual charter schools in Michigan relative to traditional public schools in their districts, finding that a quarter of all charter schools had student enrollments that were at least 20 percent out of racial balance with their respective districts.

More recently, using student-level data from North Carolina, Bifulco and Ladd (2006) examined charter school choice patterns and found that black students are more likely to migrate to charter schools with higher concentrations of black students than are enrolled in their exiting schools. They found a similar pattern for white enrollment: "One key finding is that both black and white charter school families tend to choose schools with peers who are more similar to their own children racially and socioeconomically than would be the case in their regular public school" (Bifulco and Ladd, 2006, 26). They also concluded that "the racial- and class-based sorting of students across charter schools in North Carolina has increased racial segregation, has contributed to the poor performance of charter schools and has widened the black-white test score gap" (4). Booker, Zimmer, and Buddin (2005) used individual-level data from Texas and California and found similar results: "Black students in particular tend to move to charter schools that have a higher percentage of black students and are more racially concentrated than the public schools they leave" (22).

Hastings, Kane, and Staiger (2005) examined choice patterns in Charlotte, North Carolina. Their study focused mainly on student achievement levels, finding choice patterns whereby high achievers are much more influenced by school achievement scores than are low scorers. The racial element to this is not a focus of the study, but the authors note a correlation coefficient of .65 between student test scores and the percent of African Americans at a school. In terms of the *de facto* segregative effects of choice, this suggests a dynamic where African American students are relatively likely to remain in their neighborhood schools, while white students are relatively likely to actively choose a school—and that school is relatively likely to already have a high concentration of white students. This is consistent with earlier research by Smrekar and Goldring (1999), who found that parents with more education and higher income tended to use a wider array of resources than low-income parents when choosing a school.

In one of the few studies to show an integrative effect from school choice, a case study of San Diego's choice patterns found that students, including African American students, tended to choose schools with higher white enrollment than the schools they leave (Betts et al., 2006). But the authors note that San Diego's choice system includes a voluntary busing and integration program, and they further note that this program does more to integrate students than does a simple open enrollment plan.

In perhaps the most definitive research thus far, Saporito and Sohoni (2006) analyzed national data sets and found that school choice added to racial segregation—beyond the segregation attributable to housing patterns. They linked maps of school attendance boundaries with 2000 census data, the Common Core of Data, and the Private School Survey for the 22 largest U.S. school districts. Like Betts and his colleagues (2006), they found that San Diego and a few other districts that had tied race-conscious desegregation policies to their choice policies did succeed in reducing racial segregation, but the overall effect of choice was segregative.

Importantly, these studies do not attribute choices to any given motivation. Howe and his colleagues (2001), for instance, note that the segregation patterns they describe are associated at least as much with student test scores as with race. These studies do, however, point to a self-reinforcing process, with higher-scoring schools enrolling increasing numbers of high-scoring students, and lower-scoring schools losing those higher-scoring students. This stratification pattern is mirrored in racial enrollment patterns. Whatever the parental choice motivations, the resulting *de facto* racial patterns are nonetheless evident.

Whether the long-term effects of choice in a given school district mirror the short-term segregative effects indicated by these studies would depend, in part, on whether that choice system changes schooling options such that white families opt into that district's schools. That is, white families may be attracted to a district because of its choice options. On the other hand, the pattern shown by research on choice and segregation suggests that these white families would be disproportionately opting into majority-white schools. Both points, however, are speculative—that white families would be attracted to the district by choice options, and that the choices made would perpetuate patterns of segregation—and await empirical investigation of the long-term effects of choice.

Most of the above studies concern public school choice, particularly charter schools, and these policies are not means-tested. In contrast, because existing voucher programs generally are means-tested and thus limit eligibility to low-income students, many concerns about stratification are lessened. As McEwan puts it, "Cream-skimming might occur in some instances, but the skimming is done from a decidedly small bottle" (2004, 69). Others have pointed to empirical studies to argue that means-tested voucher programs simply do not skim. Peterson (2001), for example, contends, "In general, little evidence exists that voucher programs either skim the best and brightest students from public schools or attract only the lowest-performing students. On the contrary, voucher recipients resemble a cross section of public school students, though they may come from somewhat better educated families."

The GAO's analysis agreed that voucher families, as compared to a random sampling of public school families in their home school district, did have lower income and were more likely to be headed by single parents (GAO, 2001, 13). However, the GAO also concluded that parents in these voucher families tended to be more educated. Given that these families were filtered through means-testing, their higher level of parental education might initially seem surprising. As a practical matter, however, a key additional filter that exists in all choice programs effectively selects for parental involvement in their children's education—a factor highly correlated with parental education.

Accordingly, extant research points to a possible pattern showing, in comparison with neighboring public school families, little or no cherry-picking of means-tested voucher recipients by such factors as test-scores, family income, single-parent households, and race. However, one can expect greater participation among eligible children whose parents have more education and are more engaged in their children's education. In particular, patterns of stratification by parents' education level and involvement may appear *within* the means-tested eligible subpopulation. For programs without means-testing, most notably the neovoucher policies in Arizona and Georgia, one can expect such stratification by parental education but one can also expect stratification by income, race, and correlated factors.

It should be noted that, notwithstanding some wariness about the potential for voucher programs to increase segregation in public schools, they also have the potential to lessen the racial isolation of the voucher students themselves—to remove these students from segregated public schools and place them into more integrated private schools. This appears to have happened in Cleveland and in Milwaukee (see discussion in GAO, 2001, 20–22; see also Coons and Sugarman, 1978, and Howe, 1997, for discussions of vouchers' potential to advance equity).

Conclusion

Overall, the research concerning vouchers should give pause to those who would look to market-based educational approaches to treat what ails American schooling. The combination of stratification plus few or no achievement or competition benefits leaves little (other than ideological preference) on which to hang one's policy hat. Yet means-tested voucher and neovoucher policies also have only a minimal downside. Stratification due to disparate parental efficacy only takes place within the means-tested parameters, and those who do take advantage of the choice are generally happy that they did. Within this indeterminate research context, neovouchers (tuition tax credits) have nonetheless gained traction.

The next chapter broadly discusses tax incentive approaches to providing assistance for the education of students in such schools, tracing the evolution of the tax policies that preceded the current proposals.

Notes

1. A variation on this idea is found in federal Coverdell Education Savings Accounts, which give parents tax-free investment income. These are discussed in chapter 3.

2. As discussed in chapter 4, Puerto Rico adopted this type of tuition tax credit law in 1995, two years before Arizona. However, it was not successful.

3. Maine and Vermont also have publicly funded voucher programs for students in small towns and rural areas, but all participating schools must be nonreligious. Similarly, the extremely limited and short-term Alum Rock voucher experiment in the early 1970s did not involve religious schools (Weiler, 1974).

4. A fourth voucher-like plan in Florida targets funding for private companies to provide online educational resources (*St. Petersburg Times* Editorial Board, 2006).

This relatively small program ($7.2 million as of 2006) pays approximately $5,200 per student, meaning that it provides funding for almost 1,400 students. The policy was dubbed the "virtual voucher" and the "Bennett voucher" by the *St. Petersburg Times*—the latter because former U.S. Education Secretary William Bennett lobbied for it and gained an initial state contract for his company.

5. Arizona, Colorado, Georgia, Louisiana, Ohio, and Utah have also passed voucher laws. However, at least two of these laws have not survived. Colorado's law was found to be in violation of the state constitution's local control provision (Welner, 2004). In 2005, Utah passed a voucher law that, like Florida's McKay Scholarships, focuses on special education students, and Arizona (2006) and Georgia (2007) soon followed. Similarly, Ohio in 2003 adopted a voucher plan for children with autism, and Arizona (2006) adopted a program targeted at foster children. Utah in 2007 also adopted a more expansive voucher law, but it was rejected only months later by a statewide referendum (Gehrke, 2007). In addition, Arizona's two targeted voucher laws were found by a state court of appeals in May of 2008 to violate the Arizona Constitution because public money was allocated to help private and religious schools (Davenport, 2008). Most recently Louisiana passed a voucher law in June 2008 for a limited number of lower-income students in New Orleans (Barrow, 2008).

6. Any given corporation may not take a credit for more than 75 percent of taxes due, and may not contribute more than $5 million to any single Scholarship Funding Organization.

7. See also Hess (2002), Sawhill and Smith (2000), and Teske and Schneider (2001).

8. See (for Dayton) Peterson, Greene, Howell, and McCready (1998); Howell and Peterson (2000); West, Peterson, and Campbell (2001); and see (for Washington DC) Peterson, Greene, Howell, and McCready (1998); Wolf, Howell, and Peterson (2000); and Wolf, Peterson, and West (2001). Executive summaries for these and other papers from the Peterson group are available at www.ksg.harvard.edu/pepg/execsum.htm.

9. See Peterson, Myers, Haimson, and Howell (1997); Peterson, Myers, and Howell (1998); Myers, Peterson, Mayer, Chou, and Howell (2000); and Mayer, Peterson, Myers, Tuttle, and Howell (2002).

10. See (for Milwaukee) Witte (1997, 1998, 1999, 2000); Witte and Thorn (1996); and Witte, Sterr, and Thorn (1995); and (for Ohio) Metcalf (1999, 2001); Metcalf and Legan (2006); Metcalf et al. (1998a, 1998b, 2001, 2003a, 2003b). Another evaluation of the Milwaukee program was recently conducted by the legislature's audit bureau (Wisconsin Legislative Audit Bureau, 2000).

11. See (for Milwaukee) Greene, Peterson, and Du (1997, 1998) and (for Cleveland) Greene, Howell, and Peterson (1998, 1999).

12. In addition to the claim of no significant positive effects, a small amount of evidence indicates that vouchers may be associated with academic losses for some recipients (Bracey, 2003).

13. In the original analysis, race was assigned only according to the racial/ethnic category of the student's mother.

14. For a further discussion of statistical approaches to the data, see Barnard et al. (2003), which includes comments and rejoinders.

15. Lubienski and Lubienski (2006b) responded with a harsh assessment of Peterson's approach. Readers should, however, resist viewing this simply as an impenetrable critique and counter-critique—the reports and arguments are set forth in easily understandable terms and should be considered on their respective merits.

16. Hoxby rejected this explanation, calculating that "the voucher students' departure would raise fourth grade scores in Milwaukee public schools by at most one point in language and two points in math and science" (Hoxby, 2003a, 36).

17. To be no longer categorized as failing, a school was required to pass any of the three sections on the Florida test—reading, math, or writing.

18. Supporters of vouchers have also pointed to a recent article from Rajashri Chakrabarti (2008), who was a post-doctoral scholar working at Paul Peterson's Program on Education Policy and Governance at Harvard. She argues that voucher programs that increase competitive effects by threatening public schools with the loss of revenue are more successful at improving public schools.

3

Preferring Preferences

Taxes as Policy Instruments

Tax laws are key policy documents. They directly reflect governmental priorities, providing incentives and disincentives for taxpayer behavior. Policymakers change tax laws in order to promote home ownership, retirement savings, and other actions determined to be beneficial.

Quality education for the nation's children is undoubtedly of sufficient importance to merit such a policy intervention. But policymakers have disagreed vehemently about how best to pursue this goal. One such disagreement concerns the question of whether the governmental role should be limited to maintaining a public school system, or if governmental assistance should be provided for non-public education. The tax question is subordinate; among those who want to extend assistance to non-public education, many policymakers wonder why they should turn to tax incentives when a direct allocation will serve the same purpose. For them, the question becomes: *Why, when, and how should such a tax incentive policy be conceived?*

I leave for later chapters a discussion of the merits of governmental support for nonpublic schools. In this chapter, I instead discuss the nature and history of tax incentive approaches to providing assistance for the education of students in such schools.

The Tax Expenditure Doctrine

Taxes exist primarily to fund governmental services. For instance, if the government wants to provide rental housing assistance to the poor, it can levy a tax to raise the revenue and then use that money to pay landlords for so-called Section 8 housing.[1] But taxes do more than just raise money. Whether government so intends or not, "[t]axes change people's behavior and influence the economy by altering incentives to work, consume, save, and invest" (GAO, 2005, 1). Taxes on food are low because it is a necessity; taxes on cigarettes and alcohol are higher because policymakers are relatively comfortable with the idea of placing a disincentive on such purchases.

Tax deductions and tax credits are essentially adjustments to the amounts that taxpayers otherwise must pay to the government. By changing the amount owing if the taxpayer engages in a particular action or makes a particular investment, such policies move resources toward favored destinations. If the government wants to subsidize home-ownership for the middle class, one possible approach (the one not taken) would be to levy a general tax and then target the revenue to home purchases made by the middle class—in much the same way that it funds Section 8 housing for the poor. Instead, the approach taken by the federal government has been to provide a tax deduction for interest paid on mortgages for owner-occupied homes. Under either approach, the governmental policy enlarges the market and creates greater housing opportunities. In both cases, too, the policies come with a price-tag; both reduce the size of the available tax-generated revenue. In 2001, for instance, the federal mortgage interest deduction resulted in $65 billion of tax revenues being "diverted to subsidize owner-occupied housing, compared with $14 billion [spent on Section 8] rental vouchers" (Burman, 2003, 622).[2]

Because tax deductions and tax credits (and other tax treatments, such as exemptions) have these bottom-line similarities to direct expenditures, the federal government began in the late 1960s to keep an accounting of so-called tax expenditures. As explained by Stanley Surrey, the assistant secretary of the U.S. Treasury for Tax Policy under President Johnson and the person credited with creating the tax-expenditure doctrine:

> The tax expenditure concept posits that an income tax is composed of two distinct elements. The first element consists of structural provisions necessary to implement a normal income tax, such as the definition of net income, the specification of accounting rules, the determination of the entities subject to tax, the determination of the rate schedule and exemption levels, and the application of the tax to international transactions. The second element consists of the special preferences found in every income tax. These provisions, often called tax incentives or tax subsidies, are departures from the normal tax structure and are designed to favor a particular industry, activity, or class of persons. They take many forms, such as permanent exclusions from income, deductions, deferrals of tax liabilities, credits against tax, or special rates. Whatever their form, these departures from the normative tax structure represent government spending

for favored activities or groups, effected through the tax system rather than through direct grants, loans, or other forms of government assistance. (Surrey and McDaniel, 1985, 3)

This doctrine and its underlying concept, equating a tax expenditure to a direct expenditure, was a crucial point of contention in the legal challenge to Arizona's tuition tax credit law. As discussed in chapter 5, the majority of the Arizona Supreme Court rejected the doctrine. Based on that rejection, the court concluded that a provision in the state's constitution prohibiting funding of religious institutions is not applicable to a tax credit. That is, even if the provision would have prohibited a direct governmental expenditure, it does not prohibit a tax credit, since the money funding the religious institutions should not be considered to come from the government (see *Kotterman*, 1999).

The two largest federal tax expenditures are the exclusion of employer contributions to medical insurance premiums and medical care ($126.7 billion) and the deductibility of mortgage interest on owner-occupied homes ($61.5 billion) (GAO, 2005, providing figures for fiscal year 2006). All together, the value of federal tax expenditures was approximately $850 billion in fiscal year 2004 (GAO, 2005). Burman (2003) lists 57 tax expenditures, each of which had a price tag of at least a billion dollars. They fell into two main categories: business tax expenditures and social tax expenditures. The investment tax credit and incentives for energy production and conservation are well-known examples of the former. They are intended "to promote investment generally or to help certain industries that Congress has considered important for economic growth or national security" (Toder, 1999). Social tax expenditures make up the larger category—those designed to further goals that policymakers have determined to be socially beneficial, such as health care, housing, retirement savings, and education.

Policymakers may favor tax deductions or credits over direct expenditures for a variety of reasons. In some cases (such as Individual Retirement Accounts), tax incentives seem to be the most straightforward way to change taxpayer priorities and decision-making. Further, some policymakers favor tax incentives simply because less money passes into governmental hands. Coming from the perspective that earnings belong to the individual, not the government, libertarians and some conservatives are inclined to favor almost any policy that reduces taxes.

Toder (1999) contends that tax expenditures are popular because they appear to be tax cuts rather than what they really are—spending increases. "Compared to direct outlay programs with similar goals, they better meet the need of politicians to appear to favor spending restraint and in some circumstances can be financed at a lower political cost" (Toder, 1999). However, he concludes with a caution to such politicians:

> Tax incentives make the income tax system more complex and make it appear less fair in its treatment of taxpayers in equal economic circumstances. They conceal the cost of program administration by adding burdens to the IRS instead of explicitly funding administration by program agencies. They allow politicians to understate the contributions of new programs to the size of government by promoting them as tax cuts instead of new spending (Toder, 1999).

In sum, tax expenditures have practical uses, but they can also be used to conceal budgetary realities that would be more straightforward if presented as a direct governmental expenditure.

Charitable Contributions to Religious Institutions

The tuition tax credit laws analyzed in this book are the descendents of the basic charitable tax deduction laws that Americans now take for granted. Just four years after the 1913 constitutional amendment allowing for a federal income tax, the War Revenue Act of 1917 was passed and included a deduction for contributions to charities serving religious, scientific, and educational purposes, among others. The law treated donations to religious institutions the same as donations to charitable institutions. That approach, as regards the tax deduction for charitable giving, has remained in place ever since.[3]

This charitable or religious contribution deduction allows a taxpayer to donate to a private, religious school and then take a deduction to reduce adjusted gross income (AGI) on federal income tax calculations. The primary difference between this and the tuition tax credit approach is that a tax credit provides a direct reduction in taxes owed. A tax deduction reduces taxable income; a tax credit provides an offset against the final tax due. For instance, if an Arizona taxpayer has $50,000 in AGI, she may owe about $1,000 in state income tax. If she donates $100 to a "school tuition organization" in Arizona, she can take a credit for the full amount, now owing only $900. If she lived in New Mexico, and if her marginal tax rate (the rate paid on each additional dollar of income) is 5 percent, then she could deduct the contribution but would only reduce her AGI to $49,900 and reduce her consequent tax burden to $995.

As a legal matter, a key difference between the broad deduction for charitable and religious donations and specific tax credits (such as for tuition) is that the latter option is targeted at a particular, favored subgroup of charitable donors. Thus, for example, the above Arizona taxpayer could not take the tax credit if she gave the $100 to her local library or museum or Red Cross—only the regular charitable deduction would be allowed.

However, the charitable deduction introduced in 1917 must also be understood as highly precedent-setting. Applying the framework discussed above, the deduction is a tax expenditure, effectively diverting government revenues into the coffers of religious institutions. As explored in chapter 7, there exist no clear lines between tax preference and direct allocation or between deduction and credit. The 1917 law opened a Pandora's box, the contents of which we may just now be noticing.

Tax Credits and Deductions for Educational Expenses

Another, more recent progenitor of the neovoucher is the tax credit or tax deduction for educational expenses. These policies allow a child's parents or legal guardians to take a tax credit or deduction for the purchase of educational resources such as extracurricular activities, transportation, books, and computers—or private school tuition. It was piloted in Minnesota, which adopted a tax deduction in 1955. The deduction was for up to $200 spent on education-related expenses, including private school tuition. The maximum deduction amount was increased in 1976 to $500 per child for elementary school expenses and $700 per child for secondary school expenses. This 1976 version of the law was upheld as constitutional by the U.S. Supreme Court in *Mueller v. Allen* (1983). The current Minnesota law was enacted in 1999, and it still allows for the tax deduction (now $1,625 for elementary and $2,500 for secondary) for private school expenses. This deduction is "above-the-line"—it can be taken by parents who use the standard deduction (that is, those who do not itemize).

The current law in Minnesota also includes a tax *credit* for educational expenses but, as opposed to the deduction, private school tuition is not eligible. Families with incomes below $33,500 can claim a credit of $1,000 per student or $2,000 per family. The credit is steeply phased out for higher-income families; it disappears when the family income hits $37,500.[4] Expenses exceeding the claimed tax credit can be used as a deduction. Importantly, the credit is "refundable," meaning that a family owing taxes in an amount less than the eligible credit will get a check from the state for the difference. For instance, a family that can claim a credit of $1,000 but owes only $400 in taxes can take the $400 credit and owe no taxes and, in addition, will receive a check from the state for the remaining $600.

As noted above, Minnesota's 1976 tax deduction program was challenged and upheld by the U.S. Supreme Court in 1983 (the case is discussed in chapter

5). The challenge to Minnesota's law, as well as the 1983 *Mueller* decision by the Supreme Court declaring the constitutionality of that law, brought a wave of attention to the issue (see Catterall, 1983; Darling-Hammond and Kirby, 1985; Glazer and Breneman, 1982; James and Levin, 1983). Tax deduction laws were analyzed as a new, constitutional way for the government to support private, religious education. Having cleared the establishment clause hurdle, these policies could be adopted throughout the country, in whichever states were politically welcoming.

Yet while proposals for such laws were common, and remain common, very few have passed. Only three states have joined Minnesota: Iowa (in 1987), Illinois (in 1999), and Louisiana (in 2008). In fact, the predictions following the *Mueller* (1983) decision—that it would usher in widespread increases in state support for private, religious schools—presaged the post-*Zelman* dynamic. Notwithstanding the predictions, neither case punctuated the pervasive adoption of reform laws. Instead, while cases like *Mueller* and *Zelman* are unquestionably landmarks, the movement toward greater state support of private, religious education has been relatively slow.

Iowa's 1987 law allowed parents to claim a tax deduction for each child's education expenses, including private school tuition. Like Minnesota, the deduction was capped at $1,000 per child. If parents did not itemize deductions, they were allowed to claim a tax credit set at 5 percent of the first $1,000 paid for each child's expenses. The credit and the deduction were both non-refundable; a parent not owing taxes received no benefit from the state. Also, the deduction and credit were only available to taxpayers with a net income under $45,000. As was the case in Minnesota, the law was subjected to a legal challenge and was upheld (*Luthens*, 1992).

Iowa's current law differs substantially from this original version. The law now allows all parents to claim a tax credit of 25 percent on their first $1,000 in education expenses for their child (or dependent)—accordingly, the credit is for no more than $250 per dependent. That is, the tax deduction has been eliminated, the 5 percent credit has been increased to 25 percent, and there is no longer an income ceiling. Again, the credit is not refundable.

The Illinois law closely resembles Iowa's. The credit can be taken against costs incurred for expenses including private school tuition; again, it is non-refundable; and again, it is for 25 percent. The tax credit ceiling per family is set at $500. This 1999 law was immediately challenged in court, and it was upheld by a state appellate court in *Toney* (2001).

The 2008 Louisiana law provides a state income tax deduction for 50 percent of private school tuition, with a comparable tax break for homeschoolers. The qualified tuition ceiling is $10,000, meaning that a parent paying $10,000 in tuition per year would be eligible for a $5,000 deduction. If the parent is in the highest state tax bracket (6 percent), the deduction would decrease taxable income by $300 per pupil.

No other state has adopted this form of tax credit mechanism, although new proposals are considered across the nation each year. In recent years, the states considering proposals have included New York, Indiana, and South Carolina (see Soifer, 2006). In addition, various federal proposals are considered each term by the U.S. Congress, which passed a related policy signed by President Bush in 2001—Coverdell Education Savings Accounts that allow parents to make annual contributions of up to $2,000 into investment accounts. Income earned on these accounts is not taxed, so long as distributions are put to certain qualified uses, including certain elementary and secondary education expenses at public, private, or religiously affiliated elementary or secondary schools.[5]

The Double Tax Burden Rationale

The policy rationale underlying these education tax credit and deduction laws is straightforward: no parent should have to pay twice for the education of her child (Boaz and Barrett, 1996; HSLDA, 2004). That is, a parent who decides to homeschool or to send her child to a private school incurs various costs. She also pays taxes, which support public schools in her district and state (and throughout the nation). Her neighbor, who sends his child to public school, also pays taxes but he actually gains the advantage of those taxes. He uses the services. So he only pays once for his child's education, while she pays twice—once to support a public service that she has opted not to use and once for the private education that she has chosen. A tax credit or tax deduction can help to mitigate that second payment.

This rationale implicates some core philosophical issues about the role of public education in American society. A child's education is a private good, of value to the child and the child's parents. But that child's education is also a public good, with a value to the community and society. The health of America's democracy and economy is powerfully affected by the nature and quality of K-12 education. Accordingly, all taxpayers contribute to that education. This includes parents of public school students, although they do not contribute those taxes directly to the education of their own children. Similarly, parents of private school students contribute, as do parents of homeschooled students. Grandparents also contribute. Non-parents and parents of adult children carry the same burden. From this perspective, the parent of a child in private school does not in fact pay twice for her child's education, because her taxes should not be considered as payment for the education of her own child.

By analogy, consider the shopper at Barnes & Noble who feels entitled to a tax deduction because she already paid taxes that went to fund the local public library. Or consider the subscriber to a home security service who wants a deduction because her taxes already fund the local police department. The recent increase in the number of toll highways might lead to commuters on those roads seeking a tax break because they have already funded the non-toll highway system. In each case, the taxpayer can legitimately contend that the public service purchased with tax money did not meet her needs, so she again had to pay for those services, this time on the private market.

These analogies do not, however, completely mirror the private school situation. Perhaps most importantly, schooling decisions for one's child sometimes implicate deeply held religious values. Instruction in American public schools cannot be grounded in religious beliefs. That is, although a public school education can be supplemented with religious teaching in the home and church, the public education itself is essentially secular. For some religious parents, this is insufficient. If one believes that all knowledge arises out of a given faith, then teaching knowledge (and values) apart from that faith is false and even heretical. This sets the schooling decision apart from, for example, a decision to use a toll road. Accommodation of diverse religious beliefs and practices is a core American principle, embodied in the "free exercise clause" of the First Amendment (see the discussion in chapter 5). The freedom of parents to opt for private schooling or homeschooling is an example of how the government achieves that accommodation. Another example concerns the current tax treatment of religious institutions, providing tax deductions for charitable donations and exempting church property from taxation. A third example differs from state to state, but involves the provision of publicly funded services to children attending nonpublic schools (e.g., special education services). The new tax credit and tax deduction laws that recognize the financial baggage associated with the decision to opt out of public schooling are arguably another aspect of accommodation.

From the perspective of many civil libertarians, policies such as these conflict with the establishment clause's dictate against government benefits for religion. However, if one's perspective is that "the power to tax involves the power to destroy" (Chief Justice Marshall in *McCulloch*, 1819, 431), then these laws merely fulfill the free exercise dictate against burdening religious freedom.

Given this tension and the importance of each policymaker's perspective, government neutrality toward religion is an aspiration—a goal to strive for but one that is not realistically attainable. Stephan Carter (1993) gives the example of an Alabama law allowing schools to mandate a one-minute period of time, before the school day begins, for "meditation or voluntary prayer." This law was held by the U.S. Supreme Court to violate the establishment clause (*Wallace*, 1985) because it created a coercive environment promoting student prayer. Carter writes:

> And what are the likely classroom dynamics [created by the law]? I have nothing on which to base an empirical judgment, but I can hazard an educated guess. Many students *will* pray—we can take that as given—but if the effect on the dissenter of silent prayer during a moment when all students are silent is as coercive as the majority feared, then the Court is probably wrong to suggest that, in the absence of the moment of silence, nothing prevents those students who want to pray from doing so. After all, if the knowledge that many of one's classmates are praying during the moment of silence produces pressure to pray (and the Court may be right), then surely the knowledge that many of one's classmates are *not* praying as the school day opens will produce pressure *not* to pray. There is, in short, no neutral position. (191)

Faced with this sort of dilemma, vouchers and tax credits offer an attractive alternative. Instead of trying to fit all schools to all children, they facilitate each family's ability to choose an appropriate school. This is particularly salient in the area of religious teaching, since the establishment clause prohibits public schools from providing the religious education that many parents want for their children. Tax credits and vouchers offer a loophole, allowing the government to assist all parents in funding their children's education, even if those parents' educational decisions are driven by religious beliefs. The next chapter examines the realization of this idea, in the form of neovouchers: tuition tax credits designed to mirror the effects of vouchers.

Notes

1. Section 8 is a federally funded program that provides housing vouchers to low-income families to help them pay for rental housing (and sometimes for mortgage payments) in the private market (42 U.S.C. § 1437f).

2. Burman adds that two other programs helped low-income renters: "$6 billion for public housing, and $3 billion for the low–income housing tax credit." However, looking at the larger picture also uncovers an additional major benefit for the middle and upper class: "[a]nother $22 billion in assistance for homeowners was conveyed via the deduction for property taxes" (Burman, 2003, 622).

3. U.S. Code, Title 26, Subtitle A, Chapter 1, Subchapter B, Part VI, Sec. 170.

4. The $37,500 increases slightly when families have more than two children. For instance, a family with four children would be eligible until their income reaches $43,500.

5. Some have also argued that the federal tax deduction for payment of interest on home mortgage has school choice implications. "These deductions act to subsidize the cost of families exercising their choice to reside in desired school districts or attendance areas, which often have higher property values and higher amounts of deductible local property taxes or home mortgage interest payments" (Smole, 2003, 2).

4

Current Knowledge on the Nature and Effects of Neovoucher Policies

F̲OR ADVOCATES OF GOVERNMENTAL SUPPORT for nonpublic schools, tax deductions and credits such as those described in the previous chapter accomplish quite a bit. They have the potential to extend governmental assistance to families that might consider homeschooling or private or religious schools. They also play an important symbolic and political role, essentially recognizing the legitimacy of governmental support for these schooling choices. However, these policies also come up short in a fundamental way. Ever since 1955, when Milton Friedman put forward the concept of universal vouchers—of a market-based funding plan reliant on parental choice and giving no advantage to public schools (even, perhaps, eliminating public schools)—that model has stood as an ideal among privatizers. Policies providing tax deductions and tax credits for individual expenditures lack a real potential to transform the education system. As Professor Friedman explained in his seminal treatise, *Capitalism and Freedom*, the governmental role should be only to ensure "that the schools met certain minimum standards . . . much as it now inspects restaurants to insure that they maintain minimum safety standards" (Friedman, 1962, 89; see also Friedman, 1955). Accordingly, from this perspective government should not run schools. Tax policies that provide some aid to families who choose nonpublic schooling may be a step in the right direction, but it is hard to imagine such policies being scaled up to the extent that they would change the nation's educational system to the profound extent envisioned by Friedman.

Professor Friedman's voucher concept—which indisputably does carry this potential to transform the educational system—has gained sporadic traction. Perhaps most notably, General Augusto Pinochet's government in Chile embraced the idea, at the urging of President Nixon (see Hsieh and Urquiola, 2003; McEwan and Carnoy, 2000). But as set forth in chapter 2, the number of publicly funded vouchers in the United States is still relatively low; legal and political obstacles have been prohibitive. Now, however, neovoucher policies have emerged as a way to bridge the gap between vouchers on the one hand and individual tax deductions and credits on the other. These new policies essentially create vouchers without a direct governmental expenditure, a distinction which (as discussed in chapters 5 and 6) has potentially decisive legal and political implications.

The structure and specifics of neovoucher laws can (and do) vary. Using the laws in Arizona, Pennsylvania, and Florida as primary case studies, this chapter examines several possible variations on the tax credit theme and explores the likely effects of such laws. Because each of these three states has largely eschewed evaluations and has otherwise failed to demand data from participants in their policies, the analysis in this chapter is necessarily piecemeal. Yet by drawing upon diverse sources it quilts a revealing patchwork of information.

Tuition tax credit policies like those in Arizona, Pennsylvania, and Florida have prompted various descriptions, many of them uncomplimentary. They have been called a "shell game" and "money laundering" (Moskowitz, 2006, quoting a New Hampshire Republican representative), based in part on the intricate pathways described in chapter 2. The policies have also been called "back-door vouchers" (Erdley, 2004). All of this is, of course, political rhetoric. But, setting aside the derisiveness of "back-door," this last statement is also largely accurate. A voucher is simply a certificate that is exchangeable for a future expenditure, for cash, or for some other benefit. Nothing in this definition requires that a voucher entail a direct governmental expenditure. Accordingly, the privately funded plans in New York City and elsewhere are accurately called voucher plans, as are the tax credit policies in states like Arizona. They are most accurately described as tax-credit-funded vouchers. Former Florida governor Jeb Bush refers to them as "tax credit vouchers" (Bush, 2007). In this book, I refer to them as "neovouchers" or "tax credit vouchers," which distinguishes them from the two other policies: vouchers directly funded by the government and tax credit policies providing benefits for individual educational expenses.

The Three Laws

The neovoucher laws in Arizona, Florida, Georgia, Iowa, Pennsylvania, and Rhode Island share a basic structure and intent, but they also have significant

TABLE 4.1
Comparison of Established Neovoucher Laws

State	Arizona	Pennsylvania	Florida
Year Enacted	1997	2001	2001
Eligibility for, and Amount of, Tax Credit	Individuals owing income tax to the state may claim 100% of a donation of up to $1,000 per taxpaying couple. No ceiling on the total amount of donations or credits allowed. Corporate plan added in 2007 (not described here).	Corporations may claim a tax credit on 90% of a donation,* up to $200,000 annually. There is a $54 million cap on total credits allowed ($35.9 million for the private school component)—awarded on a first-come, first-served basis until the cap is hit.**	Corporations owing income tax to the state may claim 100% of any contribution, so long as they do not contribute more than $5 million to any one organization. The total amount of tax credits statewide is capped at $118 million per fiscal year.
Eligibility for Neovoucher	At discretion of School Tuition Organization (STO). Earmarking allowed if not for own dependant.	Maximum family income is $50,000 plus $10,000 for each dependent member of the household. For instance, a family with four dependent children and income under $90,000 would be eligible. No earmarking allowed.	Students must qualify for free and reduced-price lunch and must have (1) attended public school full time during the previous year, (2) received a scholarship from an eligible organization during the previous school year, or (3) be eligible to enter kindergarten or first grade. No earmarking allowed by taxpayer, but SFO can apparently earmark.

(*continued*)

TABLE 4.1
(*continued*)

Non-discrimination Provisions	The law prohibits the recipient schools from discriminating "on the basis of race, color, handicap, familial status or national origin."	The nonpublic school must comply with Title VI of the Civil Rights Act of 1964.	The nonpublic schools must also comply with federal anti-discrimination provisions, must meet state and local health and safety laws, and must comply with all state laws regulating nonpublic schools.
Number of Participating Students (2007–08)	27,153	44,000***	19,416
Amount of Neovoucher	At discretion of the STO; no floor or ceiling.	At discretion of the Scholarship Organization (SO); no floor or ceiling.	The voucher amount may not exceed $3,950.
Public Schools Aspect	A 100% tax credit for donations of up to $400 per taxpaying couple is available for donations to public schools, to support extracurricular activities.	More than one-third of donations must go toward funding innovative educational programs for public school students.	Donated money may be used by the Scholarship-funding Organization (SFO) to subsidize transportation to an out-of-district public school.

Sources: Each state's respective statute, Enlow (2008) and United States Department of Education (2007).
* For a one-year commitment, the tax credit is for only 75% of the donation; for a two-year commitment, the credit is for 90%.
** Pennsylvania also has a 100% tax credit for donations to organizations granting "scholarships" to private pre-kindergartens, capped statewide at $5 million annually.
*** Data include pre-K students

differences.[1] Table 4.1 presents those similarities and differences, focusing on the established laws in Arizona, Florida, and Pennsylvania.

As set forth in the following discussion, each of these three state policies has been the subject of a small but important body of research. I will first present the relatively extensive research done in Arizona, followed by a description of the little we know about the policies in Florida and Pennsylvania. The new laws in Iowa, Rhode Island, and Georgia as well as the ground-breaking policy from Puerto Rico, are briefly discussed at the conclusion of this chapter.

Arizona

Arizona's neovoucher law originally allowed for a state tax credit of up to $500 per taxpaying couple for donations to school tuition organizations (STOs), which would then allocate vouchers to parents. Beginning in tax year 2006, this amount was increased to $1,000. As was briefly explained in chapter 2, the tax credit is dollar-for-dollar, covering 100 percent of the donation. Arizona essentially tells individuals who owe state taxes that they may reallocate that money from the state general fund to an STO, to be passed along to a private school. As described below, Arizona added a second neovoucher plan in 2006, allowing for credits to corporations that make donations to STOs. Arizona's Democratic governor, Janet Napolitano, vetoed four different bills attempting to create this corporate neovoucher law before finally letting SB 1499 become law in March of 2006 as part of negotiations to work out a compromise budget with the state's Republican legislature (Scutari, 2006).

The older Arizona law, geared toward individual taxpayers, places only a few limitations on those involved in its tuition tax credit system. The tax credit is, for instance, "not allowed if the taxpayer designates the taxpayer's donation to the school tuition organization for the direct benefit of any dependent of the taxpayer" (A.R.S. § 43-1089(E)). However, although Arizona bars the earmarking of a donation to one's own dependent, there is no prohibition against earmarking in favor of, for instance, a non-dependent grandchild. Further, the law allows donations that designate the schoolmate or neighbor of one's child. And, in fact, according to an article in the *Arizona Republic*, this has given rise to strategic dealing: "Parents are writing $500 checks for their friends' kids and asking them to do the same for theirs" (Bland, 2000, A22). The newspaper identified one STO for which 96 percent of all donations were earmarked for specific private school students. Even though the Arizona law appears to allow this sort of targeted donation, the practice is arguably in violation of federal law, which prohibits charities from offering *quid pro quo* benefits to donors or their friends (Lips, 2003).[2]

That said, no prosecutions or other enforcement appear to have taken place.

A second limitation found in the Arizona law is simply a provision that prohibits recipient schools from discriminating "on the basis of race, color, handicap, familial status or national origin" (A.R.S. § 43-1089(G)(2)). Note that the law does not address discrimination based on religion, which would implicate the core mission of many private schools. The same is true of the laws in Pennsylvania and Florida, which only require participating schools to comply with federal anti-discrimination statutes; religious discrimination is not prohibited. Moreover, in contrast to laws and rules governing most public schools, the neovoucher laws allow for students to be rejected or dismissed based on academic performance or behavioral issues.

The final limitation requires that each Arizona STO be associated with at least two schools. For larger STOs set up to serve a group of schools, this is not a concern. For instance, the Catholic Tuition Organization of Phoenix (CTOP), the STO formed by the Roman Catholic Diocese, would serve multiple schools even without the legal provision. A solitary private school's STO would, however, have to associate itself with a second school. Yet this provision, too, has only limited effectiveness—to the extent that its goal is to distribute funding broadly. As the dissenting justices noted in the Arizona Supreme Court case that upheld the constitutionality of the law, while the law prohibits the STOs "from making grants to 'only students of one school,'" the statute does not prevent an STO from directing all of its grant money to a group of schools that restrict enrollment or education to a particular religion or sect" (*Kotterman*, 1999, 626). That is, "nothing forbids an STO from limiting its grants or scholarships to students who adhere to a particular religion and will participate in the required religious observance" (*Kotterman*, 1999, 626). This enables the formation of STOs devoted to the support of a particular religious belief.

In fact, groups like the Arizona Christian School Tuition Organization (ACSTO) formed in order to target taxpayer-donors interested in supporting scholarships to schools with particular beliefs (in this case, evangelical Christianity). Further, even though the STOs cannot completely control recipient-parents' school choices, they can target parents based on their knowledge of those parents' inclinations. CTOP, mentioned earlier, requires that recipients be enrolled in a Diocese school (Lips, 2003). The president of the ACSTO, when asked if the group had ever had a parent not choose a Christian school, responded that this had never happened: "I don't know what we'll do when we see that," he said. "The people coming to us know who we are and that we're interested in giving scholarships to kids to go to these schools" (Schnaiberg, 1999).

In addition, what the dissenting judges in the *Kotterman* case did not realize at the time is that an STO could, in fact, give to just one school. "While the law states that scholarship organizations cannot designate the money to benefit students of only one school, the organizations do not actually have to give out scholarships for more than one school. In other words, as long as they list more than one school as possible scholarship recipients, then they are in compliance with the law" (Snell, 2002). In 2005, Christ Lutheran School Foundation handed out 69 vouchers, totaling $114,230; all of this money went to students attending a single school (Arizona Department of Revenue, 2006). Similarly, the Arizona Lutheran Scholarship Organization gave 43 vouchers, totaling $61,688, all to students attending just one school (Arizona Department of Revenue, 2006).

An unrelated recipient issue was uncovered by a reporter for the *Arizona Republic* (Kossan, 2007). Rainbow Acres, which provides a home for mentally disabled adults, created something they called "Rainbow Academy," which received almost $200,000 in neovouchers from a particular STO. Even though the Arizona policy is clearly designed for students in primary and secondary (K-12) school, those involved with Rainbow Acres defended their use of the neovouchers, explaining that the instruction provided to the mentally disabled adults enrolled in the program is at the K-12 level. They also said that state officials had called this a "gray area." When asked by the *Republic's* reporter, Arizona Department of Revenue officials pointed out that they have no "authority or resources to track whether donations made through the law are used appropriately." But the Department's chief economist called the practice "ridiculous."

Such issues and the earmarking of recipients, discussed above, raise questions about whether benefits of the law are reaching those for whom the law was intended and those who are most in need. In particular, without requirements or incentives that direct money to low-income families, to whom are donors and STOs likely to contribute? Keep in mind that, along with the new Georgia law, Arizona's individual (non-corporate) neovoucher policy stands alone among all voucher laws in that eligibility is neither means-tested nor targeted at an at-risk population such as students with special needs (note, however, that some STOs, including CTOP, have chosen to disallow earmarking and to means-test their voucher recipients). Wealthy students can and do receive grants; in fact, the state's wealthier students appear to be receiving the vast majority of the law's benefits (Bland, 2000; Wilson, 2000, 2002). This is as true of the donations to the state's public school fund (a tax credit set forth in a companion law) as it is of donations to the private school funds (Bland, 2000; Wilson, 2002).

In addition, students who began in nonpublic schools are fully eligible to receive these Arizona grants. That is, the Arizona law includes no requirement that the recipients switch from public to nonpublic schools. Calculations from Arizona's Goldwater Institute, the organization that arguably has lobbied the hardest for neovoucher policies in that state, estimate that only 2,263 out of 19,373 scholarships in 2002 were used by switchers (Lukas, 2003). This amounts to under 12 percent.

Lukas (2003) also provides some contextual information that is helpful in understanding the actual impact of these policies: "Arizona has roughly 44,000 private school students. More than 19,000 students received scholarships in 2002, which means that roughly 43 percent of all private school students received some tuition assistance through the scholarship tax credit program" (16). These numbers indicate that this policy is very effective at reaching private-school families. The neovouchers help them pay tuition. However, the policy does not appear to prompt many families to switch from public to private school, nor does it appear to assist the most needy families. Lukas asserts that approximately 10 percent of private school students are eligible for free and reduced-price lunch. These low-income families were undoubtedly among those who received neovouchers, but it is equally likely that many were not. This is consistent with Wilson's (2002) conclusion that the tax credit laws in Arizona play out to the benefit of wealthy families, who are the likely donors as well as the likely recipients. The donor half of this issue is explored in greater depth in chapter 6.

The existing data and research from Arizona do not, however, provide insights into many key issues. We do not know, for instance, whether families who receive neovouchers and actually do switch from public to private schools gain academically or otherwise. Neither STOs nor schools are required to provide data that would allow such evaluative judgments. The voucher research presented in chapter 2 indicates that policies such as these are not likely to result in a practically significant change, positive or negative, in academic achievement. However, all of the voucher policies that have been studied are effectively means-tested; Arizona's higher-income beneficiaries may fare differently.

The discussion of donors in chapter 6 highlights another area of missing data. STOs are not required to provide information such as the income level of donors, nor does the Arizona Department of Revenue provide this data. Similarly, no recipient information is available other than that volunteered through surveys of STOs (see Lukas, 2003). Related to this dearth of data about donors and recipients is the guesswork about how much programs like Arizona's actually cost (or save) the state. Summaries of that guesswork are included in chapter 6, as well as some additional guesswork of my own.

In an attempt to address some information needs, Arizona amended its neovoucher law in 2003. STOs must now annually provide a report stating the number and amount of contributions received, the number of children awarded scholarships, the dollar amount of scholarships, and the names of schools that received those scholarships (A.R.S. § 43-1089(F)).

These same reporting requirements were included in the state's new corporate neovoucher law adopted in 2006. But, in other respects, the two Arizona laws include meaningful differences. In fact, the new corporate neovoucher law resembles Florida's law (which is discussed in the next section) more than it does Arizona's older law. Donors, for instance, cannot earmark in favor of specific students. The STOs must means-test voucher recipients; families must be within 185 percent of the federal poverty level established for receipt of free or reduced-price lunch (a family of four would need a combined income of $50,000 or less to qualify). The recipients must also be switchers, either moving from public to private school or entering kindergarten. Moreover, the private schools receiving voucher students must make public the school's aggregate scores on a nationally standardized, norm-referenced test. There is a maximum amount of each voucher: $4,200 for K-8 students and $5,500 for 9-12 students (with each figure increased by $100 per year, after 2006). The law originally set a ceiling of $5 million for total annual corporate contributions (which would be eligible for the 100 percent tax credit), but just three months later this ceiling was raised to $10 million (Sherwood, 2006).

Interestingly, and unlike the earlier neovoucher law in Arizona as well as the laws in Florida and Pennsylvania, the new Arizona corporate neovoucher law includes no pretense of a public school aspect. That is, nothing in the new law offers any direct benefits or potential benefits to students remaining in public schools. The major concession that Governor Napolitano did receive from the legislature was a so-called sunset clause. The corporate neovoucher law will be automatically repealed after five years if lawmakers do not otherwise act (Scutari, 2006). One would expect, however, that by 2011 the law will have a strong political constituency—a beneficiary class including private schools and their students' families, as well as some corporate donors.

Notwithstanding that sunset clause, the general trend in Arizona is clearly toward expansion of neovouchers. To illustrate that growth, consider again the two STOs mentioned earlier: the Catholic Tuition Organization of Phoenix (CTOP) and the Arizona Christian School Tuition Organization (ACSTO). In the first year of the Arizona neovoucher policy (1998), the ACSTO raised over $500,000, second in the state only to the CTOP, which raised more than $837,000 (Schnaiberg, 1999; Center for Market-Based Education and the Goldwater Institute, 2000). By 2007, the ACSTO donation total had increased to $11.3 million and the CTOP checked in at $10.7 million (Arizona Department of Revenue, 2008). Overall, $1.8 million was raised in 1998 by a total of 15 STOs (Center for Market-Based Education and the Goldwater Institute,

2000), over $13.3 million was raised in 1999 by a total of 29 STOs (Bland, 2000), and over $54 million was raised in 2007 by a total of 55 STOs (Arizona Department of Revenue, 2008; U.S. Department of Education, 2007).

Florida

Florida's neovoucher policy includes only corporate taxpayers. They are offered a dollar-for-dollar tax credit for donations to Scholarship-funding Organizations (SFOs), which then package the donations into vouchers. Each corporation may contribute up to $5 million to any given SFO, but the total amount of tax credits statewide is capped at $118 million per fiscal year.

In contrast to the initial neovoucher law in Arizona, Florida's law was expressly designed to benefit students most in need. Florida restricts recipients to only those children who qualify for free and reduced-price lunch and only those children who are switchers from public school (or are entering kindergarten or first grade). Each voucher can be for an amount up to $3,950.

According to statistics from the Florida Department of Education, students receiving neovouchers in 2006–07 attended primarily religious schools (84.5 percent). Most were students of color—24 percent Hispanic and 40 percent African American (Florida Department of Education, 2007a, 2007b; see also Hoxby and Murarka, 2006). Most were also in grades K-4 (60.7 percent of all recipients) as of October of 2007 (Florida Department of Education, 2007b). This last characteristic of the program may be because private school seats are more widely available in elementary grades. It may also be because of the law's "switcher" requirement, which includes the key exception for students eligible to enter kindergarten or first grade.

A provision in Florida's law states that SFOs may use donated money, at their discretion, to subsidize transportation for eligible public school students to an out-of-district public school. However, this provision has had little practical effect. In 2002–03, for example, only 107 public school students received this transportation funding, compared to 19,206 who received scholarships to attend a private school (Florida Senate Committee on Education, 2003, 2).

Until reform legislation (discussed below) was passed in 2006, SFOs were essentially unregulated, and an initial shake-out period saw the largest SFO, called FloridaChild, discontinue operations after discovery of some "irregularities" involving the unlawful charging of administrative fees to applicants and schools (Gallagher, 2003, 14–15). Currently, just three SFOs administer the donations in Florida, and just two administer 95 percent of all vouchers (Florida Department of Education, 2007b). Accountability and oversight issues have, in fact, dominated policy discussion about Florida's neovoucher policy since its inception. This is in part because very little data exist to explore basic implementation issues. It is also in part because the plan includes means-testing, thus obviating to some extent research questions about who is receiving the voucher—questions explored by researchers such as Wilson (2002) in Arizona.

But some high-profile problems with the program undoubtedly represent the primary reason for this focus. In 2006, reform legislation (Senate Bill 256) was passed to address issues of fraud and lack of accountability in the neovoucher plan. The reform added financial oversight to the policy, as well as a limited amount of academic assessment (Miller, 2006a, 2006b). This legislation was prompted, in part, by two reports issued in 2003—one from the state's Senate education committee and the other from the state's chief financial officer (Florida Senate Committee on Education, 2003; Gallagher, 2003).

These reports documented a lack of oversight by the Department of Education and the Department of Revenue, resulting in several embarrassing incidents. An SFO administrator was convicted of stealing over a quarter million dollars from the program (Erdley, 2004; Miller, 2006b).[3] A private school principal was accused of stealing both neovoucher and McKay Scholarship funds by falsely claiming higher numbers of enrolled students and by submitting scholarship applications falsely stating school tuition to be substantially higher than the actual tuition (Moore, 2008). The founder of another private school receiving neovoucher money—the Tampa-based Islamic Academy of Florida—was revealed to be under investigation by federal authorities as the North American leader of Islamic Jihad, a Palestinian terrorist group (Florida Senate Committee on Education, 2003; Mator, 2006). A corporation was approved as an SFO even though it was incorporated in Colorado (out-of-state incorporation is disallowed) and had even been administratively dissolved (Florida Senate Committee on Education, 2003). And, as noted above, the SFO that was initially the state's largest had to discontinue operations because it had improperly charged administrative fees to applicants and schools.

Financial irregularities and poor documentation of student enrollment also plagued the program. Only students in low-income families technically qualify, but SFOs sometimes failed in their obligation to regulate eligibility (Gallagher, 2003). SFOs also transferred money among themselves, thus possibly circumventing a provision in the law that limits the amount that any given corporation may contribute to any single SFO to no more than $5 million. As Gallagher (2003) notes, "In theory, the $5 million limit can be exceeded since the identity of scholarship funds with respect to individual contributors cannot be distinguished within a single bank account" (6).

The reports also identified a couple of practices that seemed troubling even if not inconsistent with the law's provisions. The report from Florida's chief financial officer suggested that the legislature "consider adding a statutory provision so that scholarships granted under the Corporate Tax Credit Program cannot be combined with the McKay or Opportunity Program scholarships. During the review, we noted examples where students received both McKay and Corporate Tax Credit scholarships" (Gallagher, 2003, 5). In addition, the Senate report pointed out that the law included "no state-mandated academic accountability requirements" and therefore that "the state does not know if the program is adequately serving participating students" (Florida Senate Committee on Education, 2003, 7). The report continued, "If a student fails to make adequate progress and returns to the public school system, the state and the student would be at a disadvantage" (7).

This same report discussed a possible loophole concerning earmarking. The Florida law expressly prohibits earmarking by taxpayers. The SFOs, however, are allowed to openly designate a particular child or private school for receipt of a scholarship (Florida Senate Committee on Education, 2003). The Senate report points out that this loophole could "allow a taxpayer to make a contribution to a specific scholarship-funding organization knowing which children would benefit from the contribution" (6).

Another part of the law that does not appear to be playing out as originally conceived concerns the requirement that 5 percent of the allotted tax credits for a given year be set aside for small businesses. According to Robert Ducasse of the Florida Department of Revenue, small businesses are generally not participating in the program; large corporations are the ones making the donations (Ducasse, 2005). In fact, for each of the first four years, the cap was reached with only approximately 100 corporations having donated: 77 in 2002, 114 in 2003, 102 in 2004, and 97 in 2005.[4]

The 2006 reform law addressed some, but not all, of these concerns. It includes oversight provisions that should cut down on check forgery and on students being incorrectly counted as enrolled in schools. Another provision will help to prevent neovoucher money going to school operators with criminal histories. In addition, schools receiving this money are now required to have an actual physical location where students attend regularly and meet with teachers, and these schools will be subject to random site visits (Miller, 2006b). Perhaps most importantly, students receiving neovouchers must now be given standardized tests. A compromise was agreed to whereby these students' test scores will not be used for any school reports that are released to the public (in contrast to the use of tests given to Florida's public school students) but will instead only be given to the students' parents and an independent evaluator (Miller, 2006b).

These new data should help to answer some questions. Certainly, the currently available data are extraordinarily limited, allowing for little more than speculation about the nature, motivations, experiences, and outcomes of the students receiving neovouchers. The SFOs and private schools had, for the first four years of the program, been allowed to operate with very little oversight or data collection, leaving questions raised but not answered. The reform legislation will help, but only incrementally in some key areas. For instance, the new testing requirement allows the private school to administer any "nationally norm-referenced tests identified by the [Florida] Department of Education"—the FCAT taken by public school students is not required.[5] Depending on the number and nature of tests identified, the evaluator is unlikely to be able to make valid comparisons between these test scores (and schools), or between the voucher recipients and comparable public school students.

In addition, recall the data showing that 60.7 percent of Florida's neovoucher recipients were enrolled in grades K-4, which strongly suggest that many of the recipients have not attended public schools for a substantial amount of time. This in turn suggests that voucher recipients are not so much fleeing from bad experiences at public schools as seeking out good experiences at private schools. Little or nothing in the new reform legislation will add insight to this area of inquiry.

Pennsylvania

Pennsylvania's system mirrors Florida's, except that the tax credit offered is only for 75 percent of a donation, or for 90 percent if the corporation commits to donations for two years. Pennsylvania's policy also differs from those in Florida and Arizona in that it guarantees that public school students are also supported by the donations. One-third of all donations must go toward funding innovative educational programs in public schools. (An innovative academic program is defined in the statute as "an advanced academic or similar program that is not part of the regular academic program of a public school but that enhances the curriculum or academic program of the public school" [P.S. § 20-2002-B].)

The family-income restriction in Pennsylvania's law is more generous than the one in Florida in that it encompasses middle-class families. A single-child family would be eligible so long as the family income remains under $60,000, and this limit increases by $10,000 for each additional dependent member of the household.

Although not as controversial as in Florida, some issues of reporting and accountability have arisen in Pennsylvania. The Department of Community and Economic Development (DCED), under the current Democratic governor, has clashed with the Republican legislature over these issues. The DCED had pro-posed requiring the Scholarship Organizations (SOs)—Pennsylvania's version of Arizona's STOs and Florida's SFOs—to submit an end-of-year report on their activities and information about scholarship recipients' previous school enrollment. The legislature responded in July of 2005 by passing a law (SB 507) requiring only that each SO report its total received contributions, the total number of recipients, and the total amount donated.[6]

Accordingly, the level of oversight for recipients of this funding is very low, and the information available from Pennsylvania remains very sketchy. Until the new reporting requirements were passed in 2005, no reliable numbers were available even concerning the basic question of how many students re-ceived the tax credit vouchers.

Regarding the question of who these students are, the *Morning Call* news-paper analyzed state records and concluded that although "supporters pitched the program as a way for students to escape bad public schools . . . there's no evidence that is happening" (Averett and Wilkerson, 2002). The reporters spoke with private school officials who "said that most of the scholarships are going to students already in their classrooms, in part because businesses who donate money can specify the schools that receive them. Further, a number of those schools are in affluent and middle-class areas, rather than areas where neediest students tend to live."

Similarly, the *Pittsburgh Tribune-Review* conducted their own research and reported that, as of the summer of 2004, nearly $7 million of the $100 million donated for neovouchers went to the state's "priciest prep schools" (Erdley, 2004). With regard to the public school component of the law, this reporter described a similar phenomenon, showing resources going to wealthy schools and districts (Erdley, 2002b). In order to receive donations, a school district must generally set up an educational improvement organization, which is es-sentially a non-profit foundation that accepts donations. As has been the case in Arizona, marketing and solicitation efforts by the public school districts are a key component of such fundraising. The creation of successful organi-zations has, not surprisingly, been more common in communities with the greatest resources.

The number of SOs in Pennsylvania is large—176 in 2007–2008 (Enlow, 2008). They are allowed to keep up to 20 percent of donations to pay for administrative costs (P.S. § 20-2002-B). Florida's SFOs, in contrast, are required to pass through all donations to voucher recipients (Fla. Stat., § 220.187(4)(e)), and only three SFOs now exist. These two features (number of organizations and payment for an organization's administrative costs) are probably connected. Arizona's policy finds a middle ground; it allows up to 10 percent for administrative costs (A.R.S., § 43-1089(G)(3)), and the state had 56 STOs in 2006–2007 (United States Department of Education, 2007).

Iowa, Rhode Island, and Georgia

As discussed in chapter 3, Iowa has long allowed a non-refundable tax credit for educational expenses, including private school tuition. That credit is currently set at 25 percent of the first $1,000 in expenses. In 2006 Iowa also joined Arizona, Florida, and Pennsylvania in creating a neovoucher program, as did Rhode Island. Two years later, Georgia adopted a policy that rivals Arizona's in its scope and free market characteristics. Because these three programs are just now being implemented, there is currently little in the way of results to delve into. But the differences between these new laws and the others are nonetheless instructional (see Iowa Code § 701-42.30 in appendix D, Rhode Island General Law § Chapter 44-62 in appendix E, and Georgia House Bill 1133 in appendix F).

Iowa's program resembles the original Arizona plan, in that it is available only to individuals, not corporations (and in that the nonprofits are also called STOs). In addition, the Iowa STOs are allowed to keep up to 10 percent of donations to pay for administrative costs, and each STO must serve at least two schools. However, unlike the Arizona plan, there is no public school aspect—no comparable donation opportunity to benefit students who remain in public schools. Also unlike the Arizona plan, the tax credit is not dollar-for-dollar; it is for 65 percent of the donation. Another difference is that the Iowa plan is means-tested, although the income level for eligibility extends all the way up to 300 percent of the federal poverty level.

Two other differences between the Iowa and Arizona neovoucher policies are worth noting. The Iowa plan forbids the earmarking of donations. And the Iowa plan places a cap on the total annual tax credits allowed. For 2006, the cap was set at $2.5 million; for subsequent years, it is set at $5 million. Also, while the legislation mirrors the other states' in its avoidance of the word "vouchers," it also eschews the currently favored term "scholarships," opting instead for the accurate and politically neutral "tuition grant."

Future analyses of the Iowa experience should have some data to work with. The law requires STOs to file annual reports revealing the total number and amount of contributions received, the total number and value of tuition grants, the total number of children awarded grants, the names of schools that received those grants, and the number of students and amount sent to each school, as well as an itemized list of donor and amount donated (Iowa Code § 42.30(7)).

Rhode Island's new law takes the corporate route, and it closely follows Pennsylvania's approach. In particular, the tax credit offered is only for 75 percent of a donation, or for 90 percent if the corporation commits to donations for two years. The law even borrows the Pennsylvania name (scholarship organizations) for the nonprofits that receive donations. But unlike the Pennsylvania law, the new Rhode Island law does not include a public school component.

The law does not forbid earmarking, but it does include a means-testing provision: eligible families must be within 250 percent of the federal poverty line. Also, each SO must serve at least two schools. Any given corporate taxpayer can annually take a maximum credit of $100,000, with a statewide cap on credits of one million dollars.

The Rhode Island law places on the state division of taxation a reporting requirement that is probably the most extensive among the six states with the neovoucher laws. The division must annually report the number of scholarships given by each SO overall and by recipient school, the dollar range of those scholarships, a breakdown by zip code of the place of residence for each student receiving a scholarship, and a description of all criteria used by the SO in determining to whom scholarships are awarded.

The newest neovoucher law is in Georgia, adopted in 2008. The law closely resembles Arizona's in several key respects: it provides the tax credit to corporations as well as individuals, it is dollar-for-dollar, it is not means-tested, each student scholarship organization must serve at least two schools, the law does not forbid earmarking except for one's dependent, and the credits are for up to $1,000 for individuals ($2,500 for married couples).[7] Differences with Arizona include the overall ceiling of $50 million combined credits (corporate and individual), the lack of a public school component in Georgia's law, and the requirement that recipient students start off enrolled in public school (or be K or pre-K).

Puerto Rico

School choice advocates in Puerto Rico succeeded in gaining passage of both a voucher law and a neovoucher law; neither law, however, has survived court scrutiny. The voucher law was passed in 1993, providing parents having annual incomes of less than $18,000 with vouchers for up to $1,500 toward tuition at the public, private, or parochial school of their choice. However, the Puerto Rico Supreme Court ruled in 1994 that this voucher program violated Article II, Section 5 of the Puerto Rico constitution, which provides that "no public property or public funds shall be used for the support of schools or educational institutions other than those of the state" (*Asociación de Maestros v. Torres*, 1994).

In 1995, the Puerto Rico legislature responded by establishing the Educational Foundation for the Free Selection of Schools, Inc., a nonprofit corporation that mimics the old voucher law and provides financial aid for elementary and high school students in public, private, or parochial schools. Donors to the foundation were eligible for a tax credit up to $250 for individual taxpayers or $500 for corporations and partnerships.

The government apparently helped to fund the foundation through direct allocations but also ran workplace fundraising activities, with employees asked to donate. This process did not continue, however, after the director of a government-operated group home for children won a lawsuit alleging that she was fired when she refused to contribute (*Acevedo-Delgado v. Rivera*, 2002). Although her supervisors claimed other reasons for the firing, she introduced evidence that they had told her to either contribute or submit her resignation. In the absence of compelled contributions, the foundation did not survive: "Paralyzed by court battles and debt, the foundation's offices are closed and its phones disconnected" (Roman, 2000).

Conclusion

Of the seven jurisdictions with tuition tax credit policies discussed in this chapter, only Puerto Rico and Arizona have seen legal challenges. Most notably, the plaintiffs who successfully challenged Florida's direct voucher law have thus far decided—for a combination of political and legal reasons—against a challenge to the (much larger) neovoucher law. The next chapter explains the legal issues surrounding vouchers in general and tuition tax credits specifically, focusing in particular on the possibility that the circuitous structure of tax credit laws may allow them to survive legal scrutiny even in states where voucher laws are found to be unconstitutional.

Notes

1. The full text of the statutes from Arizona, Florida, and Pennsylvania appear in appendixes A, B, and C, and are summarized in table 4.1. The text of new neovoucher laws in Iowa, Rhode Island, and Georgia are presented in appendixes D, E, and F, respectively.

2. Similarly, parents of private school students in Ohio have enrolled their children in low-performing schools, with no intent for their children to ever attend those

schools, in order to become eligible for the new, statewide voucher program (Richards, 2006). The Ohio program provides vouchers to students enrolled in public schools deemed failing for two years in a three-year period.

3. This conviction was overturned on appeal because the court found the law to have been so poorly written that the state could not prove that it had a legal right to the money (Dáte, 2007).

4. From data provided by the Florida Department of Revenue on December 8, 2005.

5. Part of the logic here is that the FCAT is aligned to the state's curriculum standards and, unlike the state's public schools, the private schools attended by neovoucher recipients are not required to teach those standards.

6. The most recent legislative activity, in July of 2007, increased the funding cap for the private school component of the program from $29.3 million to $35.9 million.

7. For corporations, the cap is 75 percent of that corporation's state tax liability.

5

Taxing the Establishment Clause

Exploring the Constitutional Issues

VOUCHERS HAD LONG FACED A DAUNTING LEGAL OBSTACLE. In 1947, the U.S. Supreme Court described a "wall of separation between church and state" (*Everson v. Board of Education of the Township of Ewing*, 1947, 16), invoking the now-famous phrase that Thomas Jefferson had used in a letter to a colleague explaining the First Amendment's establishment clause (*Reynolds v. United States*, 1879, 164). This interpretation of the establishment clause held sway for a half century, during which time public assistance to private, religious schools was kept within limited, constrained boundaries. Yet the Supreme Court gradually chipped away at the wall of separation, and the First Amendment obstacle to vouchers was finally removed by the Court's decision in *Zelman v. Simmons-Harris* (2002). As a practical matter, the same decision cleared the way for neovoucher laws.

But both policies—vouchers and neovouchers—still face legal challenges grounded in state constitutions. Under the American federalist system, a state law can be held unenforceable if it violates either the federal constitution or that state's own constitution. This chapter begins with an overview of federal law through *Zelman* and then goes on to explore legal challenges based on state constitutions, focusing in particular on the possibility that neovouchers may pass constitutional muster even in states where direct vouchers are found to be unconstitutional. If this eventuality occurs, it is likely to prompt a further political shift by choice advocates who see a viable alternative in this new approach to vouchering.

The Establishment Clause Pre-*Zelman* Precedent

The First Amendment begins by decreeing that "Congress shall make no law respecting an establishment of religion." The "no law" wording is absolute; it contemplates neither a balancing of this interest with others nor a nuanced implementation. Moreover, the clause forbids more than the establishment of religion by the federal government. It forbids even laws "respecting" an establishment of religion. Yet this clause, like much of the U.S. Constitution, is open to a great deal of interpretation—and, reflective of this ambiguity, establishment clause jurisprudence has shifted and adapted over time.

The provision of K-12 education was not among the itemized powers consigned to the federal government by the Constitution, meaning that states retained responsibility in this area. As explained by James Madison in Federalist No. 45:

> The powers delegated by the proposed Constitution to the federal government are few and defined. Those which are to remain in the State governments are numerous and indefinite. The former will be exercised principally on external objects, as war, peace, negotiation, and foreign commerce; with which last the power of taxation will, for the most part, be connected. The powers reserved to the several States will extend to all the objects which, in the ordinary course of affairs, concern the lives, liberties, and properties of the people, and the internal order, improvement, and prosperity of the State (Madison, 1778).

As written, the First Amendment applied only to Congress, not to the individual states. In fact, a state-supported church (Congregationalist) existed in Connecticut until 1818 and in Massachusetts until 1833. This inapplicability of the First Amendment to the states meant that states were not restricted with regard to the role of religion in publicly funded education. Since the establishment clause applied only to federal actions, and since the federal government was not engaged in policies regarding education, jurisprudence in this area remained undeveloped.

However, the Supreme Court held in 1947 that the establishment clause is one of the liberties protected by the Fourteenth Amendment's due process clause, which does apply to states and their subdivisions such as cities and school districts; the states, therefore, became bound by this restriction (*Everson*, 1947). When a court finds that a state or local action violates the establishment clause, the court is really finding a violation of the Fourteenth Amendment's due process clause, into which establishment clause rights are now understood to be incorporated. The extension of establishment clause protections to the actions of states has greatly increased the amount of establishment clause litigation over the past half-century.

Everson involved a New Jersey program that reimbursed parochial school parents for school transportation costs. The Court's opinion included the following passage:

> The establishment of religion clause means at least this: Neither a state nor the federal government may set up a church. Neither can pass laws that aid one religion, aid all religions, or prefer one religion over another. Neither can force a person to go to or to remain away from church against his will or force him to profess a belief or disbelief in any religion. No person can be punished for entertaining or professing religious beliefs or disbeliefs, for church attendance or non-attendance. No tax in any amount, large or small, can be levied to support any religious activities or institutions, whatever they may be called, or whatever form they may adopt to teach or practice religion. Neither a state nor the federal government may, openly or secretly, participate in the affairs of any religious organizations or groups and vice versa. In the words of Jefferson, the clause against establishment of religion by law was intended to erect "a wall of separation between church and state " (*Everson*, 1947, 15–16)

The Court added that this "wall must be kept high and impregnable" (*Everson*, 1947, 18). Yet, notwithstanding this powerful language, the decision was issued against the plaintiff, thus upholding the challenged program. In fact, the decision established the now-crucial distinction between aid provided directly to religious schools and aid provided to children or their parents—as in the *Everson* case and the recent *Zelman* case—to be used according to their own choice. The former type of allocation is generally prohibited under the First Amendment; the latter type is generally permitted.

Between 1947 and 1971, a variety of governmental programs and policies were found by the federal courts to be in violation of the establishment clause as it was construed by the Court in *Everson*. In *Abington Township School District v. Schempp* (1963), for example, the Court struck down a Pennsylvania law requiring Bible reading as part of the official curriculum. But the Supreme Court had not yet enunciated a clear set of rules to guide other, lower courts in these cases. Such rules were finally set forth in *Lemon v. Kurtzman* (1971), in which the Court struck down a state program providing aid to private, religious elementary and secondary schools. A law, the Court explained, violates the establishment clause if it fails any of three parts (or "prongs") of the following test: (1) the law must serve a secular purpose; (2) its principal or primary effect must neither advance nor inhibit religion; and (3) it must not foster an excessive government entanglement with religion. Until recently, the Supreme Court and lower federal courts applied this so-called *Lemon* test to virtually all establishment clause cases. In *Stone v. Graham* (1980), for instance, the Court applied *Lemon* and invalidated a Kentucky law requiring the posting of a copy of the Ten Commandments on the wall of each public classroom.

In cases involving governmental support for private, religious schools, the first "prong" of the test has been easily satisfied: a secular purpose of such aid is to help families pay for their children's education. For instance, in *Committee for Public Education v. Nyquist* (1973), the Court accepted that New York programs providing aid to private schools and parents of private school children had secular purposes such as protecting the health and safety of private school students and assisting overburdened public schools that might otherwise then have to educate those private school children.

The final two *Lemon* prongs are the ones that have tended to be most at issue in cases involving governmental support for private, religious schools. The entanglement prong focused attention on the difficulty of ensuring that public money is spent only on the nonreligious education components within a private, religious school—the concern being that governmental strings and supervision will necessarily follow the public funding. (This issue is explored in greater detail below, in connection with the *Aguilar v. Felton* [1985] case.) The remaining *Lemon* prong requires that a law be neutral toward religion both on its face and in its application and that the law not have the primary effect of advancing the sectarian aims of nonpublic schools (see *Mueller v. Allen*, 1983, 392; see also *Nyquist*, 1973, 788; *Witters v. Washington Department of Services for the Blind*, 1986). As we will see, this primary-effect inquiry has become the main focus of recent school support cases.

The Supreme Court modified the *Lemon* test in its 1997 decision in *Agostini v. Felton*. It kept the "purpose" prong but combined the other two. That is, the Court created a modified effects test by combining the "effects" and "entanglement" prongs of the old *Lemon* test. The key modification was that entanglement alone would not result in a finding of unconstitutionality. Instead, the Court identified three primary criteria that it would consider together in determining whether a government action has a primary effect of advancing religion: (1) government indoctrination, (2) defining the recipients of government benefits based on religion, and (3) excessive entanglement between government and religion (*Agostini*, 1997).

This change allowed the *Agostini* to uphold the constitutionality of New York City's program sending public school teachers into parochial schools to provide Title I reading services. The Court had earlier, in *Aguilar* (1985), held this same program unconstitutional because of the excessive entanglement associated with the school district's strict guidelines for ensuring that the assistance not be used to further private schools' religious teaching. Among other precautions, teachers were instructed to avoid involvement in religious activities and were to avoid instructional use of any religious materials. Moreover, the school district sent out supervisors to each school once every month to check up on the Title I teachers and report their findings to an even higher administrative level. The *Agostini* Court again took note of these entanglement concerns, but it then also noted that the program did not lead to governmental indoctrination, nor did it select particular students based on religious affiliation. Instead, the primary effect of the policy was to enhance a child's secular education, while neither advancing nor inhibiting religion.

This decision in *Agostini* unquestionably smoothed the way for *Zelman* (2002) five years later; but there were important differences between the New York City program in the former case and the Cleveland voucher program in the latter. New York's program provides educational services directly to parochial and private school children, services that they might not otherwise receive from their nonpublic schools. The added instruction does not relieve these private schools from any educational services they must already provide nor does it provide any public funding for these schools. Any indirect benefit to the private school (as opposed to the private school students), such as improved overall student achievement, would be incidental to the program and would occur regardless of whether the instruction occurred on or off school grounds. Voucher programs, on the other hand, are designed to channel public funding to private schools, aiding their ability to fund core, regular expenses such as equipment purchases, faculty salaries, and facilities maintenance.

The Court's Shifting Concerns

The evolution of the U.S. Supreme Court's approach is illustrated by a comparison of two earlier cases, *Nyquist* (1973) and *Mueller* (1983), both of which ruled on the constitutionality of state tax laws providing support for private schooling. The Court in *Nyquist* struck down a New York law imparting, among other things, two benefits: (1) tuition grants to low-income families (vouchers redeemable only at private schools), and (2) tax deductions for tuition payments. The law provided no benefits for families choosing to keep their children in public schools. Noting that the private schools in New York were predominantly religious, the *Nyquist* Court stated that the grants violated the establishment clause because they were "offered as an incentive to parents to send their children to sectarian schools by making unrestricted cash payments to them" (*Nyquist*, 1973, 786). The Court explained that the law would be unconstitutional "whether or not the actual dollars given eventually find their way into the sectarian institutions. Whether the grant is labeled a reimbursement, a reward, or a subsidy, its substantive impact is still the same" (*Nyquist*, 1973, 786). As later characterized by the Court in *Mueller*, the New York law provided "thinly disguised 'tax benefits,' actually amounting to tuition grants, to the parents of children attending private [mostly sectarian] schools" (*Mueller*, 1983, 394).

In *Mueller* (1983), however, the Court upheld a similar Minnesota tax deduction, for school expenses incurred on behalf of children attending elementary or secondary schools. The law allowed parents to claim a tax deduction for elementary school expenses up to $500, with $700 allowed per child for secondary school expenses. For public school students, these expenses included textbooks and transportation expenses. For private school students, these expenses included such items plus tuition.[1]

The *Mueller* Court held that these deductions did not violate the establishment clause. Applying the *Lemon* test, the Court explained that the programs had at least two secular purposes: ensuring that Minnesota's citizenry is well educated and (more tenuously) ensuring that private and parochial schools' financial health remains sound. Further, the *Mueller* Court held that these deductions did not primarily advance the sectarian aims of parochial schools and did not excessively entangle the state in religion. In reaching these conclusions, the Court focused heavily on distinct characteristics of the Minnesota law: (a) it was open to all parents incurring educational expenses, including those whose children attend public school; and (b) the funds did not go directly to the private schools but rather reached those schools as a result of the numerous private choices of individual parents.

Although factual distinctions arguably separate these two cases, the obvious reason for the different outcomes is that the Court's membership had undergone a conservative shift.[2] Only one justice (Powell) signed on to both majority decisions. A further conservative shift accompanied the different decisions in *Aguilar* (1985) and *Agostini* (1997). By 1997, only three justices remained from the 1985 Court, with Justices Rehnquist and O'Connor moving from dissent to majority and Justice Stevens moving from majority to dissent. That is, no justice signed on to both majority decisions. As the membership of the Court became more accommodating to government support for religious institutions, the decisions followed. The new Court majority was now receptive to laws that would have been held unconstitutional in 1973 or even 1985.

Current Establishment Clause Jurisprudence

When considering establishment clause issues, the predominant approach for justices on the current Supreme Court focuses on the idea of governmental neutrality. Under this approach, the clause prohibits the government from acting non-neutrally, by preferring one religion over another, or by promotion of, or hostility to, religion in general. The majority opinion in *Zelman* (2002) applies this neutrality test. However, it should be noted that some justices have continued in recent years to apply the *Lemon-Agostini* test, and two justices—O'Connor and Kennedy—also have applied their own particular approaches. Justice O'Connor applied what some call the "endorsement test," asking whether a reasonable observer is likely to draw an inference that the government is endorsing a religious practice or belief (see *Mitchell v. Helms*, 2000, 843, O'Connor, J., concurring). As she explained, "The Establishment Clause prohibits government from making adherence to a religion relevant in any way to a person's standing in the political community" (*Lynch v. Donnelly*, 1984, 687, O'Connor, J., concurring). This endorsement test is most likely to be applied by the Court in situations where the government is engaged in expressive activities, such as graduation prayers, religious signs on government property, or religious elements of a school curriculum.

Justice Kennedy, who stands as a key swing vote in the aftermath of O'Connor's retirement, has promoted a slightly different establishment clause approach, sometimes called the coercion test (*County of Allegheny v. ACLU*, 1989, 660–61, Kennedy, J., concurring in part and dissenting in part). The government, from this perspective, does not violate the establishment clause unless it (a) provides direct aid to religion in a way that would tend to establish a state church, or (b) coerces people to support or participate in religion. In comparison to the *Lemon* test, this test is substantially less likely to result in a violation of the establishment clause. It eliminates the purpose prong and substantially reduces the entanglement and effects inquiries.

Yet questions involving use of government funds are increasingly determined by the Court (including Justice Kennedy and former Justice O'Connor) under the rubric of neutrality. This neutrality approach requires that the government treat religious groups the same as other, similarly situated groups. The Supreme Court, using this neutrality analysis, has issued decisions allowing states to provide the following: nonreligious textbooks for students in parochial schools (*Meek v. Pittenger*, 1975); reimbursement to religious schools for the grading of tests that were prepared, mandated, and administered by the state (*Committee for Public Education & Religious Liberty v. Regan*, 1980); a sign language interpreter for a deaf student attending a Catholic high school (*Zobrest v. Catalina Foothills School District*, 1993); reading teachers for low-performing students eligible for Title I services, including those students attending religious schools (*Agostini*, 1997); and computers to both religious and public schools (*Mitchell*, 2000). And, of course, neutrality reasoning was used to sanction a policy allowing religious schools to participate in a voucher program (*Zelman*, 2002).

In relevant part, the First Amendment states, "Congress shall make no law respecting an establishment of religion, or prohibiting the free exercise thereof; or abridging the freedom of speech." Neutrality cases typically implicate these free speech (and sometimes free exercise of religion) concerns, in addition to establishment clause concerns. Typical is *Widmar v. Vincent* (1981), in which the Supreme Court considered a University of Missouri policy that generally opened its facilities to the public but excluded groups engaged in religious worship. The university claimed a compelling interest to justify the exclusion—namely, an interest in complying with the restrictive, separation-of-church-and-state language of the Missouri state constitution. This language, among other things, prohibits the state from making "an appropriation or pay from any public fund whatever, anything in aid of any religious creed, church or sectarian purpose, or to help to support or sustain any private or public school, academy, seminary, college, university, or other institution of learning controlled by any religious creed, church or sectarian denomination whatever" (Missouri Constitution, Article IX, Section 8). In spite of this state constitutional provision, the Court held that the university's policy discriminated against particular, religious content, in violation of the free exercise and free speech clauses of the U.S. Constitution:

> [T]he state interest asserted here—in achieving greater separation of church and State than is already ensured under the Establishment Clause of the Federal Constitution—is limited by the Free Exercise Clause and in this case by the Free Speech Clause as well. In this constitutional context, we are unable to recognize the State's interest as sufficiently "compelling" to justify content-based discrimination against respondents' religious speech. (*Widmar*, 1981, 276)

The Court has continued to develop this neutrality principle over the past two decades. In a case similar to *Widmar*, the Court in *Rosenberger v. Rector & Visitors* (1995) struck down a policy at the University of Virginia that provided funding for nonreligious student publications but denied funding for a religious student publication. Rejecting the argument that the policy served a government interest in maintaining a strict separation between church and state, the Court explained that the "guarantee of neutrality is respected, not offended, when the government, following neutral criteria and evenhanded policies, extends benefits to recipients whose ideologies and viewpoints, including religious ones, are broad and diverse" (*Rosenberger*, 1995, 839).

The Court has taken the same stance with regard to K-12 practices. In *Lamb's Chapel v. Center Moriches Union Free School District* (1993), it invalidated a facilities-use policy comparable to that in *Widmar*. The school district had made its rooms generally available for community use but would not let the rooms be used for the showing of a religious movie. The Court held that the district could not base a denial of access on the group's religious viewpoint. This same type of so-called viewpoint discrimination was also declared unconstitutional in *Good News Club v. Milford Central School* (2001), in which the school district policy excluded a Bible study group even though it had otherwise opened its facilities to any group that wished to discuss "instruction in any branch of education, learning, or the arts" (102).

The constitutional focus of these neutrality cases, even within the religion context, has been the free speech clause (rather than the free exercise clause) of the First Amendment. The principle of non-neutrality is essentially an extension of the broader prohibition against discrimination targeting speech that is offensive to the government because of its content or viewpoint. Yet, as *Zelman* (2002) makes clear, neutrality is also a central concern for the Court's majority in establishment clause matters.[3]

Zelman v. Simmons-Harris

As applied by the majority in *Zelman* (2002), the neutrality principle concerned the evenhandedness of the state's distribution of public funding. The Court also relied upon the tenet enunciated long ago in *Everson* (1947), distinguishing between direct aid to religious institutions and indirect aid as part of a neutrally applied program whereby funding makes its way to religious institutions only through intervening choices of parents or other third parties. The Court stressed that parents in Cleveland had a variety of nonreligious choices, including choices among public schools. Accordingly, the Court characterized the funding through the Cleveland voucher plan as offered to a broad class of citizens, not just to those seeking religious options. For these reasons, the Court concluded, the program is neutral toward religion.[4]

Although the Court's interpretation of the establishment clause remains in flux, it is likely that for the foreseeable future a majority of justices will continue to view government neutrality toward religion as its guiding principle, at least in cases involving vouchers and tuition tax credits. Policymakers designing such plans therefore have approximate guidelines concerning how to write laws that will pass muster under the federal Constitution. A plan that grants parochial schools benefits beyond those granted to public schools or otherwise favors religious institutions would likely fall outside the guidelines. However, a plan that extends to parochial school students those benefits that are also offered to public school students will likely be sanctioned. Of course, advocates will have plenty of room for argument concerning where on this continuum any given voucher or tax credit policy happens to fall.

State Constitutions

The *Zelman* decision upholding Cleveland's voucher policy was followed by a flurry of pronouncements and news reports, all heralding an inevitable wave of voucher legislation (see Andrews, 2002; Paige, 2002). But as the fervor subsided, new notice was taken of state constitutional provisions—such as the Missouri provision discussed above in relation to the *Widmar* case—expressly prohibiting public funding of religious schools (see Goodstein, 2002). A law permitted under the federal Constitution may nonetheless be prohibited by a state's constitution, either because of different wording in the two constitutions or because of courts' different interpretations of the same wording. That is, although the U.S. Supreme Court's reasoning in *Zelman* may be persuasive to a state court faced with interpreting its own constitution, it is not binding on that state court.

As a practical matter, these state constitutional provisions addressing the separation of church and state were quietly sleeping in the back room for years and years until the Court's 2002 *Zelman* decision set off the alarm clock. So long as the federal establishment clause was applied using the old *Lemon* test, plaintiffs challenging the laws had little need to rely on these state provisions. And, because lawyers have only rarely relied on these provisions, courts have had few opportunities to interpret them and to specifically define which policies they allow or disallow.

Keeping in mind the undeveloped nature of this area of jurisprudence, the following description of state constitutional law begins with a general examination and then considers whether neovoucher laws may have legal advantages that make them more attractive than traditional voucher laws. As we will see,

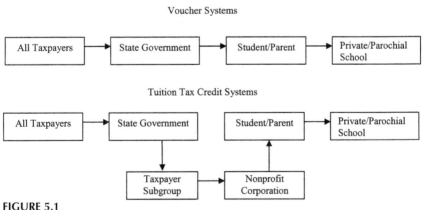

FIGURE 5.1
Comparison of Voucher and Tuition Tax Credit Systems

this analysis largely boils down to the question of whether a legally meaningful distinction should be drawn between the following two approaches:

1. A law providing for the funding of X through an expenditure of public money from a state's general fund (e.g., vouchers); and
2. A law providing for a decrease in taxes owed by a taxpayer because that taxpayer has made a private expenditure to fund X (e.g., neovouchers).

In graphical form, consider again the two pathways presented in chapter 2 (see figure 5.1). State courts will have to determine the legal implications (if any) of the more circuitous tax credit pathway.

Blaine Amendments and Compelled Support Provisions

Of the 50 state constitutions, 47 contain at least one of two different types of religion clauses, either of which may be held to prohibit voucher or neovoucher policies. The most common of these clauses is the so-called Blaine amendment, named after Maine congressman James Blaine, the initiator of a failed 1875 effort to amend the U.S. Constitution.[5] That proposed amendment would have precluded grants or appropriations to sectarian institutions or organizations. In addition to Missouri's, Blaine's language or similar wording is found in the constitutions of 35 other states, plus Puerto Rico.[6] The movement to include these Blaine amendments in state constitutions took place during the period from 1875 to 1900 and was associated with anti-Catholic sentiment, even if the motives of any given supporter may have been innocuous (see Viteritti, 1996, 144).

Eighteen of these 36 state constitutions with a Blaine amendment also include a second clause—one found in 29 constitutions overall—prohibiting the state from forcing residents to support any ministry.[7] These so-called compelled support clauses can be traced back to the governmental practice, relatively common in the colonial period, of compulsory tithing to support favored churches. Given this historical context, it is not surprising that Eastern, mid-Atlantic, and Midwest states are much more likely to have this language in their constitutions.[8]

Importantly, even though the Blaine and compelled-support wording is often very strong, any given state's courts may decide to read the language in a forgiving way, allowing vouchers or neovouchers notwithstanding the apparent prohibition (see *Kotterman*, 1999; see also the discussion later in this chapter). Only Michigan's state constitution includes language that directly and explicitly forbids vouchers and tax benefits.[9]

Tax Credit Mechanisms

The Supreme Court's holding in *Zelman,* grounded in a rationale of religious neutrality plus "genuine and independent private choice" (648), is straight-forwardly extendable from vouchers to neovouchers. All existing neovoucher laws create nonprofit organizations that receive taxpayer donations and package those donations, giving the money as vouchers for parents to use in sending their children to private schools. Several of these neovoucher laws also include provisions designed to give nominal benefits to public schools, plainly making an appeal to principles of neutrality.[10] Although every tax credit law may present unique bases for legal challenge, there is nothing in the basic structure of the tax credit system that provides a legal basis for distinguishing such policies as less neutral than vouchers or less grounded in independent private choice.[11]

Even given a federal green light, however, the religion clauses of state constitutions will continue to present serious legal hurdles for both types of policies—vouchers and neovouchers. Arizona's experience illustrates these challenges and, in addition, highlights the potential for neovouchers to survive legal challenges in states where vouchers might not. After the Arizona law was passed in 1997, it was immediately challenged in state court. One of the grounds for that challenge was the Blaine language in the Arizona constitution, which states, "No public money or property shall be appropriated for or applied to any religious worship, exercise, or instruction, or to the support of any religious establishment" (Article II, §12). In addition, "No tax shall be laid or appropriation of public money made in aid of any . . . private or sectarian school" (Article IX, §10).

Supporters of the Arizona policy argued that this language was inapplicable because a tax credit is simply not an appropriation of public money. In opposition, the plaintiffs—individuals with religious and public-school affiliations—argued that there is no meaningful difference between a formal allocation and a tax credit. As described above, the tax credit mechanism effectively offers to Arizonians who owe state taxes the option of reallocating some of that money from the state general fund to a tuition-granting organization.

Tax credit opponents' contention regarding the essential equivalence between allocations and tax credits is known in legal circles as the tax expenditure doctrine. As discussed in chapter 3, a tax expenditure is generally defined as a law providing for a tax exemption, exclusion, deduction, or credit that is designed to achieve various social and economic objectives and that results in a loss of tax revenues (Surrey, 1970). The fiscal impact on the state of a tax expenditure is largely indistinguishable from a direct expenditure of state funds.

This tax expenditure approach was rejected by the majority of a divided (three to two) Arizona Supreme Court, which reasoned as follows:

> [N]o money ever enters the state's control as a result of this tax credit. Nothing is deposited in the state treasury or other accounts under the management or possession of governmental agencies or public officials. Thus, under any common understanding of the words, we are not here dealing with "public money." (*Kotterman v. Killian,* 1999, 618)

The dissenting judges attacked this reasoning, arguing that it has little support from other jurisdictions: "Other courts, state and federal, have long viewed 'tax subsidies or tax expenditures [similar to Arizona's tax credit as] the practical equivalent of direct government grants'" (*Kotterman,* 1999, 641, quoting a Massachusetts case).

Recall the U.S. Supreme Court's description of the New York law struck down in *Nyquist* (1973): "thinly disguised 'tax benefits,' actually amounting to tuition grants, to the parents of children attending private [mostly sectarian] schools" (*Mueller,* 1983, 394). "Whether the grant is labeled a reimbursement, a reward, or a subsidy, its substantive impact is still the same" (*Nyquist,* 1973, 786). Grants "offered as an incentive to parents to send their children to sectarian schools by making unrestricted cash payments to them [violate] the Establishment Clause . . . whether or not the actual dollars given eventually find their way into the sectarian institutions" (*Nyquist,* 1973, 786). Such reasoning was dismissed by the Arizona *Kotterman* court, which focused instead on the technical fact that the taxpayers' dollars that helped to support the religious schools were never in the possession of the state.

The main critique of the *Kotterman* decision, allowing for the use of tax credits in the face of the constitutional ban on state support of religious institutions, is that it elevated form over substance. The constitution's restriction becomes virtually meaningless if it can be subverted by laundering the money through intermediaries. As discussed in chapter 7, if tax credits are not considered government allocations, then what would realistically be left of the state religion clauses? Why could a similar mechanism not be used, for example, to pay the salaries of church pastors? Why could the rationale not be used to allow positive check-offs on state and federal taxes to fund any religious institution or activity?

Another criticism, also grounded in the roundabout trip taken by the neovoucher money, is more complex but equally important. Vouchers as well as neovouchers include one type of indirect allocation: money goes to private schools only through parents. That is, the money goes first to parents and then to the schools. There is a core policy reason for this: the danger of government weighing in on behalf of a given religion or church is ameliorated when the policy shifts from a direct allocation to a set of individual allocations chosen by parents on behalf of their children. Accordingly, the insertion of parents into the allocation process has a reason other than obfuscating the true source of the allocation.

But neovouchers add a second indirect element. Instead of the government providing a voucher for parents to use, the government backfills money (through a tax credit) that is donated by taxpayers to a nonprofit. The nonprofit then provides the voucher to the parents. What, other than obfuscation, is accomplished by the addition of the complexities of neovouchers? What is added by having taxpayer donations determine who allocates the benefit to parents? There exists no sensible policy goal to buttress this aspect of the tax credit system—no policy justification for shifting this decision-making authority from parents to a relatively wealthy subset of taxpayers.

Notwithstanding this critique, the *Kotterman* decision demonstrates that neovoucher policies can withstand court scrutiny, even in states with constitutions containing Blaine language. For advocates of neovouchers, who look at the many states with this language in their constitutions, this is a major victory holding great promise. Tax credit opponents, on the other hand, can find solace in *Kotterman*'s dissenting opinion, which demonstrates that, in the minds of other judges, Blaine language can provide the grounds for striking down tax credits. Moreover, the Arizona decision is not binding on courts in other states, and the tax expenditure approach has widespread usage and support in budgetary and legal circles.[12] Accordingly, it would be reasonable to expect among Blaine states a split of legal authority—differing court decisions—as tax credit policies make their way through the courts.

While the tax credit policy survived the scrutiny of the Arizona Supreme Court, the *Kotterman* court's reasoning cannot be extended to vouchers, which are clearly funded through government revenues. In fact, the two voucher programs that Arizona had initiated in 2006—directed to public school students with disabilities and to former foster children who had been adopted—were struck down in 2008 by a state appellate court (*Cain v. Horne*, 2008). The court pointed out although the state constitution's "religion clause" could be interpreted as placing no greater limits on state action than does the federal establishment clause, the federal constitution has no wording that corresponds to Arizona's "aid clause" (its Blaine amendment language). The court did consider the *Zelman* neutrality arguments, but those arguments are a harder sell when the prohibition is not simply against "establishment" but rather against any support or aid to a nonpublic school.[13]

Other Court Interpretations of Blaine Amendments

In addition to Arizona, important decisions have been issued in several states, offering insights into how Blaine language will be applied to voucher and neovoucher laws. Wisconsin and Illinois have interpreted their state constitutional language as essentially creating the same protections and limitations as does the federal establishment clause, despite the fact that the constitutional language itself is different (see *Griffith v. Bower*, 2001; *Jackson v. Benson*, 1998; *Toney v. Bower*, 2001). However, as discussed below, the language in Wisconsin's constitution is substantially less comprehensive than the "aid clause" in Arizona's constitution.

The Milwaukee Parental Choice Program (MPCP), which began in 1989, provides vouchers to qualified students from families at or near the federal poverty level. The state sends a check directly to the school but made out to the parents, who endorse it over to the participating schools, which must first have notified the state of their intention to participate in the program. Voucher students must be excused, upon request, from the religious aspects of schooling, and the schools cannot exclude students based on religious or nonreligious preferences. At the time that the Wisconsin Supreme Court considered the law, 6,194 students were participating in the program, far below the ceiling of approximately 15,000 students technically allowed to participate.

The Wisconsin Constitution includes the following provision:

> The right of every person to worship Almighty God according to the dictates of conscience shall never be infringed; nor shall any person be compelled to attend, erect or support any place of worship, or to maintain any ministry, without consent; nor shall any control of, or interference with, the rights of conscience be permitted, or any preference be given by law to any religious establishments or modes of worship; nor shall any money be drawn from the treasury for the benefit of religious societies, or religious or theological seminaries (Wis. Const. art. I, §18).

In narrowly interpreting this provision, the state Supreme Court wrote that the crucial question under this provision, as under the federal establishment clause, is "not whether some benefit accrues to a religious institution as a consequence of the legislative program, but whether its principal or primary effect advances religion" (*Jackson*, 1998, 621, internal citations omitted). The court was essentially applying the modified *Lemon* test enunciated by the U.S. Supreme Court the previous year, in *Agostini* (1997). Foretelling *Zelman*, the Wisconsin court continued, "public funds may be placed at the disposal of third parties so long as the program on its face is neutral between sectarian and nonsectarian alternatives and the transmission of funds is guided by the independent decisions of third parties" (*Jackson*, 1998, 621).

Based on this reasoning, the Wisconsin court upheld the constitutionality of the Milwaukee voucher plan.[14] The court stated:

> In our assessment, the importance of our inquiry here is not to ascertain the path upon which public funds travel under the amended program, but rather to determine who ultimately chooses that path. . . . not one cent flows from the State to a sectarian private school under the amended MPCP except as a result of the necessary and intervening choices of individual parents. (*Jackson*, 1998, 618)

Similarly, the Arizona Supreme Court later explained that the decision-making process preceding the scholarship allocation under the tax credit law is "completely devoid of state intervention or direction" (*Kotterman*, 1999, 614):

> Arizona's statute provides multiple layers of private choice. Important decisions are made by two distinct sets of beneficiaries—taxpayers taking the credit and parents applying for scholarship aid in sending their children to tuition-charging institutions. The donor/taxpayer determines whether to make a contribution, its amount, and the recipient [School Tuition Organization]. . . . Parents independently select a school and apply to [a School Tuition Organization] of their choice for a scholarship. . . . schools are no more than indirect recipients of taxpayer contributions, with the final destination of these funds being determined by individual parents. (*Kotterman*, 1999, 614)

As described in chapter 3, Illinois enacted the old-fashioned type of tax credit law in 1999—a credit given to parents to offset educational expenses including private school tuition. This law was upheld by a state appellate court, which first rejected the tax expenditure argument and then concluded that the tax credit does not violate the religion clauses in the state constitution (*Toney*, 2001). Illinois' constitution does include an aid (Blaine) clause (article X, § 3), but the court relied on an earlier Illinois Supreme Court decision enunciating a "lockstep doctrine," holding that "the restrictions of the Illinois Constitution concerning the establishment of religion are identical to those imposed by the federal establishment clause and that any statute that is valid under that clause is also valid under the Illinois Constitution" (*Toney*, 2001, 1202). Given that the U.S. Supreme Court had held that a Minnesota tax credit law did not violate the U.S. Constitution (*Mueller*, 1983), the *Toney* court found that the Illinois law did not violate the Illinois constitution.[15]

Other state courts, however, have found the religion clauses to present a higher wall of separation than that built by the federal establishment clause (Mauro, 2002). Vermont's Supreme Court ruled that its compelled-support clause required that a state system of funding private schooling for rural students must exclude private religious schools from participation in the program (*Chittenden Town School District v. Department of Education,* 1999). Similarly, applying its Blaine provision, Puerto Rico's Supreme Court struck down a law that would have resulted in state financial support for private religious schools (*Asociación de Maestros v. Torres,* 1994; see also *Opinion of the Justices to the Senate* [Mass., 1987]).[16] Colorado's voucher law was declared by its state Supreme Court to be an unconstitutional violation of a local-control provision in that state's constitution (*Owens v. Colorado Congress of Parents,* 2004). In Florida, the statewide voucher law was found by the state supreme court to be in violation of the state constitution because it allocated public funds to support an alternative system of education, in violation of the requirement that the state provide a single system of free public schools (*Bush v. Holmes,* 2006). However, the November 2008 Florida ballot will include a measure to amend the state constitution, removing this uniformity requirement and replacing it with language requiring the state to fund free public schools "at a minimum, and not exclusively," thus essentially overturning *Bush v. Holmes* and allowing for public funding of private schools (Dolinski, 2008).

The Intersection of Federal and State Law

Constitutional (and legal) jurisprudence is hierarchical. A state law will be struck down if it is in violation of a state constitutional provision. But a state constitutional provision will be unenforceable if it is in violation of the U.S. Constitution. Advocates of vouchers and neovouchers hope that such unenforceability will be the fate of the Blaine amendments in state constitutions.

A Fourteenth Amendment equal protection violation may be found when a law is passed based upon a desire to harm a politically unpopular group, thereby placing that group at a disadvantage with regard to a government benefit. This rationale was applied by the Supreme Court in *Romer v. Evans* (1996), invalidating Amendment 2, a measure passed by Colorado voters that sought to prevent jurisdictions in the state (e.g., cities, counties, and school districts) from instituting civil rights measures against sexual-orientation discrimination. For example, the city of Denver would have been prevented from adding "sexual orientation" to its anti-discrimination policy. The Court analyzed the law as specifically targeting one group for lesser legal protection, and therefore as in violation of the equal protection clause:

> A law declaring that in general it shall be more difficult for one group of citizens than for all others to seek aid from the government is itself a denial of equal protection of the laws in the most literal sense. . . . [I]f the constitutional conception of 'equal protection of the laws' means anything, it must at the very least mean that a bare . . . desire to harm a politically unpopular group cannot constitute a legitimate governmental interest. (Romer, 1996, 633, 634, internal quotations omitted)

The same analysis could arguably be applied to Blaine amendments, which can be seen to target for discrimination those interested in religious worship, exercise, or instruction.[17] Moreover, the appearance of discrimination is heightened by the anti-Catholic history of Blaine amendments in some states. What makes this argument particularly interesting is that the idea of a strict separation of church and state has been, until recently, a longstanding interpretation of the federal establishment clause, which has no anti-Catholic taint (see, for example, *Everson*, 1947; *Nyquist*, 1973). The concept itself is quite respectable. So one question framed by such a dispute is whether—even if Mr. Blaine himself had a "bare . . . desire to harm a politically unpopular group" (*Romer*, 1996, 634)—the same is true of those who included variations on his separation-of-church-and-state language in state constitutions. The motivations of the individuals who inserted a Blaine amendment in any given state constitution are difficult, if not impossible, to know. Further, almost all the provisions have been in place now for more than 100 years, giving reformers ample opportunity to remove or change the provisions; the passive decision to retain the provisions may, in many states, be based on an acceptance of the policy notwithstanding initial motivations for adopting it. For similar reasons, the Arizona court in *Cain* (2008) refused to consider arguments about the history of the Arizona constitution's aid clause.

Ironically, school choice itself could be challenged with a similar argument—that the policies were initiated because of a desire to harm a politically unpopular group. Choice became a prominent policy in the wake of *Brown v. Board of Education*. Instead of mandating that black and white students attend separate schools, boards adopted so-called freedom of choice policies purportedly allowing all students the option of enrolling in whichever school they wished. The implicit threats aimed at any black student who would dare to cross the line were not particularly subtle (*Green*, 1968). Given this history, plus the documented segregatory effects of choice policies (see Fiske and Ladd, 2000; Cobb and Glass, 1999; Howe, Eisenhart, and Betebenner, 2001), the historical intent argument—used now as a way to promote the legality of vouchers, the most immoderate of school choice laws—arrives on the scene with somewhat ill grace.

Notwithstanding this inconsistency, an equal protection challenge waits in the wings as a potential knock-out blow to all state Blaine provisions. In fact, the issue almost came before the U.S. Supreme Court in 2004, in a challenge to a law in Washington State providing a state-funded college scholarship to high-achieving, financially disadvantaged college students. This Washington law contains an exclusion expressly denying scholarship eligibility to those students seeking a college degree in "devotional theology"—a degree for those students intending to join the clergy. This exclusion was intended by lawmakers to comply with strongly worded provisions in the state's constitution guaranteeing the separation of church and state.[18] The scholarship law was challenged, and the courts initially agreed: a federal appellate court struck the law down as a violation of the First Amendment's free exercise clause. That court reasoned that the state's constitutional provisions, while they may warn against favoring religious institutions, do not provide a sufficiently compelling justification for non-neutrality toward religion (*Davey v. Locke*, 2002, 750). The court determined that states may not disfavor religious educational options, even in the guise of traditional establishment clause concerns. It concluded that, by excluding religious institutions from receipt of state allocations, the Washington law elevated concerns about church-state separation to the point where they became viewpoint or content discrimination against religious exercise and speech (see Lupu and Tuttle, 2003).

But this decision was reversed by the U.S. Supreme Court (*Locke v. Davey*, 2004). For purposes of understanding the long-term implications of Blaine amendments on voucher and tax credit laws, the Supreme Court's decision in *Locke* is more noteworthy for what it did not decide than for what it did. For pro-voucher litigators, the most desirable outcome in *Locke* would have seen the Court turn to a broader, equal protection rationale of *Romer* (1996), which had the potential to completely prevent state courts from applying their Blaine amendments.

The neutrality rationale used by the appellate court to strike down the law was of little use to voucher advocates concerned about Blaine language in state constitutions. It is true that such a decision may have been useful in challenges to laws in two states, Vermont[19] and Maine,[20] which make voucher benefits available only to students attending secular private schools and thus denying the benefits to students attending private schools with religious affiliations. However, these Vermont and Maine laws can be distinguished from the Washington law, in that "a reasonably objective observer could believe that the state [Vermont or Maine] was applying state funds to religious instruction" (*Davey*, 2002, 760). In this regard, courts are more wary about public funding for K-12 education than for college education. Furthermore, most existing and proposed state voucher and neovoucher laws make benefits equally available for all private schools—religious and secular—meeting the same basic eligibility requirements. Because these laws themselves do nothing to disfavor religious schools, the *Davey* (2002) appellate court's neutrality approach offered no significant assistance to voucher supporters.[21]

As it happened, the Court decisively rejected the appellate court's neutrality approach, with seven of the nine justices joining Chief Justice Rehnquist's majority opinion. The Court's reasoning involved the interplay between two parts of the First Amendment—the establishment clause and the free exercise clause. The constitution forbids laws "respecting an establishment of religion or prohibiting the free exercise thereof." The establishment clause prevents, for example, public school teachers from leading a prayer. But the free exercise clause prohibits public school teachers from interfering with a student's private prayer. Both clauses protect religious freedom, but they can still come into conflict.

In general, the Supreme Court has read the two clauses together as simply requiring that the government remain neutral toward religion—not infringe on religion but also not provide it with any benefits. But how does the state draw the line with a scholarship like the one in Washington? The idea of state-supported clergy runs afoul of the establishment clause. But free exercise (and free speech) concerns are implicated by a law that singles out a "devotional theology" degree as the only type of degree that the state will not support.

The Court got around this problem by focusing on the question of whether the law's exception was an attempt to treat certain religious beliefs and choices in a hostile way—something akin to Justice O'Connor's "endorsement" test. The state's goal, the Court determined, was not to disfavor religion but rather to avoid the danger of state-supported clergy. Accordingly, the Court allowed the state to subsidize a secular activity and to exclude subsidization of a comparable religious activity.

Importantly, this distinction was allowed, not required. As the Court had earlier indicated in *Witters* (1986) and *Zelman* (2002), Washington (or any other state) would also be allowed to extend the benefit to the religious activity. The Court explained that there exists what it called a "play in the joints" between the establishment and free exercise clauses (*Locke*, 2004, 718). A state's decision to pursue the goal of separation of church and state may go beyond what is required by the establishment clause and still not violate the free exercise clause.

So where does this leave states with provisions in their constitutions like Washington's? Directly, at least, the *Locke* decision has little applicability for states considering voucher or neovoucher laws. Indirectly, however, the *Locke* decision is important for several reasons. First, it provides precedent against arguments that free exercise (and free speech) protections prevent a state (such as Maine or Vermont) from singling out religious schools, excluding them from the benefits of a voucher system. Second, the Court added to its line of cases allowing laws that tie conditions to government funding (see *Rust v. Sullivan*, 1991).²² For voucher laws, this means that participating private religious schools may find unwanted conditions attached to their receipt of the government money. Among the possibilities: no discrimination based on sexual orientation or on religion or church membership; participation in standardized testing systems; compliance with IDEA-like special education rules; and, as was recently adopted in Iowa (Robelen, 2008), curricular requirements. Third, the Court expressly chose not to address the issue of whether Washington's Blaine amendment is discriminatory and thus violates the federal equal protection clause. Instead, the Court pointed out that the Washington policy was more closely tied to the other, similar provision in the state's constitution.²³

In the wake of *Zelman* and *Locke*, one can expect somewhat different legal arguments in state court challenges to voucher laws than in such challenges to neovoucher laws. In voucher litigation, the initial arguments will likely focus on whether to limit the state provision(s) to something akin to the federal interpretation in *Zelman*. This is the argument successfully employed by defenders of the Wisconsin voucher law (*Jackson*, 1998). If this equivalency is established, then the law will survive if it meets the criteria set forth in *Zelman*. For instance, the state allocation must be made to parents, who then make independent choices that may send the money along to a religious institution (*Zelman*, 2002). However, with neovoucher litigation, this all becomes the back-up argument, relevant only if the court first determines that the system includes the allocation of public funding. With neovoucher policies, the state allocation is made to taxpayers, who in turn fund the grant-giving organizations, which then pass the money to the parents who choose a school which may or may not be affiliated with a religious organization. Because of this roundabout complexity, a court might take the approach of the Arizona Supreme Court in *Kotterman* (1999), finding that no state allocation is at issue and obviating any need to decide if the state's Blaine provision is co-extensive with the federal establishment clause.

Conclusion

The First Amendment's two religion clauses are in perennial tension with one another. Attempts to accommodate the free exercise of religion can become an establishment, and attempts to avoid establishment can infringe on free exercise. The emerging examination of state Blaine amendments, in connection with the substantially narrower interpretation of the federal establishment clause in *Zelman*, raises questions about the specific nature of this tension. In concluding that there exists "play in the joints" between the establishment and free exercise clauses, the *Locke* Court answered one of the key questions: Can a state interpret its own constitution as more restrictive than the federal establishment clause without trampling the First Amendment right to free exercise?

If states continue to pursue voucher and neovoucher policies, the Supreme Court may soon consider equal protection issues surrounding Blaine amendment challenges. The Court's decision in such a case will have powerful repercussions for those Americans living under state constitutions erecting higher walls of separation than the Supreme Court recognized in *Zelman*.

Yet the potential legal advantages of neovouchers outlined here tell only part of the story. Political obstacles standing in the way of vouchers have been at least as daunting as legal ones. The next chapter looks at the political and policy implications of the tuition tax credit approach, drawing comparisons to direct vouchers—noting advantages as well as concerns.

Notes

1. Presently, as discussed in chapter 3, this Minnesota law allows a maximum deduction of $1,625 for elementary school expenses and $2,500 for secondary school expenses. Parents who do not itemize deductions on their federal income tax forms are nonetheless eligible for this deduction. Moreover, the eligible expenses covered by the deduction have been expanded to include academic summer camps, summer school, and up to $200 of the cost of a personal computer and education software.

2. Two justices, Douglas and Stewart, had retired and been replaced by Stevens and O'Connor, respectively. Justice Stewart had voted to strike down the New York law. Justice O'Connor, in contrast, joined the majority in upholding the Minnesota law.

3. An interesting, though legalistic, distinction is evident here. Neutrality arises in a very different way in these two types of cases. In the establishment clause context, the neutrality concept is used to prevent the law from being held to violate the constitution. Legal scholars would say that the argument is used as a shield to defend against attacks on the law. In contrast, non-neutrality is a sword in the free speech context. It provides a rationale for striking down the law as unconstitutional.

4. It should be noted that the Court devoted considerable space to pointing out educational difficulties facing students in Cleveland public schools, although the Court's eventual legal reasoning did not appear to rest upon these troubles. That is, the precedential value of the case would appear to extend to laws providing vouch-

ers to students in academically high-achieving school districts as well as struggling districts.

5. In 1884, Blaine was the Republican presidential nominee and lost a close election to Democrat Grover Cleveland, whose campaign focused on Blaine's alleged involvement in unethical business dealings with the railroad industry. Cleveland's followers popularized the rhyme, "Blaine, Blaine, James G. Blaine. The continental liar from the state of Maine" (DuPont, 2002).

6. See Ala. Const. art. I, § 263; Ariz. Const. art. II, § 12 & art. IX, § 10; Alaska Const. art. VII, § 1; Cal. Const. art. XVI, § 5; Colo. Const. art. IX, § 7; Del. Const. art. X, § 3; Fla. Const. art. I, § 3; Ga. Const. art. I, § 2, para. 7; Haw. Const. art. X, § 1; Idaho Const. art. IX, § 5; Ill. Const. art. X, § 3; Ind. Const. art. I, § 6; Kan. Const. art. 6, § 6(c); Mass. Const. amend. art. XVIII, § 2; Mich. Const. art. I, § 4; Minn. Const. art. I, § 16; Miss. Const. art. VIII, § 208; Mo. Const. art. IX, § 8; Mont. Const. art. X, § 6; Neb. Const. art. VII, § 11; N.H. Const. Pt. II, art. 83; N.M. Const. art. XII, § 3; N.Y. Const. art. XI, § 3; Nev. Const. art. 11, §§ 2, 9 & 10; N.D. Const. art. 8, § 5; Okla. Const. art. II, § 5; Or. Const. art. I, § 5; Pa. Const. art. III, § 29; L.P.R.A. [Puerto Rico] Const. Art. II, § 5; S.C. Const. art. XI, § 4; S.D. Const. art. VI, § 3; Tex. Const. art. I, § 7; Utah Const. arts. I, § 4 and X, § 9; Va. Const. art. IV, § 16; Wash. Const. art. I, § 11 and art. IX, § 4, Wis. Const. art. I, § 18; Wyo. Const. art. I, § 19. See also an online map prepared by the pro-voucher Institute for Justice: www.ij.org/publications/liberty/2001/10_5_01_f.html.

7. The Vermont Constitution, for instance, contains the following clause:

That all persons have a natural and unalienable right, to worship Almighty God, according to the dictates of their own consciences and understandings, as in their opinion shall be regulated by the word of God; and that no person ought to, or of right can be compelled to attend any religious worship, or erect or support any place of worship, or maintain any minister, contrary to the dictates of conscience, nor can any person be justly deprived or abridged of any civil right as a citizen, on account of religious sentiments, or peculiar mode of religious worship; and that no authority can, or ought to be vested in, or assumed by, any power whatever, that shall in any case interfere with, or in any manner control the rights of conscience, in the free exercise of religious worship. Nevertheless, every sect or denomination of christians [*sic*] ought to observe the sabbath [*sic*] or Lord's day, and keep up some sort of religious worship, which to them shall seem most agreeable to the revealed will of God. (Vt. Const. ch. I, art. 3)

8. The three states without either Blaine or "compelled support" language are Louisiana, North Carolina, and (ironically) Maine, the state that sent Mr. Blaine to Congress.

9. "No payment, credit, tax benefit, exemption or deductions, tuition voucher, subsidy, grant or loan of public monies or property shall be provided, directly or indirectly, to support the attendance of any student or the employment of any person at any such nonpublic school or at any location or institution where instruction is offered in whole or in part to such nonpublic school students." (Michigan Const. Art. VIII, § 2)

10. Most notably, Arizona created a small tax credit for donations to public schools to support extracurricular activities (A.R.S. §43-1089.01). This public school tax credit was set at $200 for married couples filing jointly when the law was passed in 1997. It was recently increased to $300 for the 2005 tax year and then to $400 for the 2006 tax year.

11. The first post-*Zelman* test of tax credit legislation took place in federal court in Arizona. In *Hibbs v. Winn* (2004), the U.S. Supreme Court gave the go-ahead to a suit challenging the state's tax credit law under the federal establishment clause. The district court applied *Zelman* and concluded that the tax credit law had all the necessary provisions to survive under the Supreme Court's standard (*Hibbs v. Winn*, 2005).

12. In fact, the tax expenditure approach has been applied (implicitly by the majority and explicitly in a concurrence) by the U.S. Supreme Court in an establishment clause case. See *Rosenberger* (1995), 842–43 and 861 n. 5 (Thomas, J., concurring).

13. This appellate court decision was handed down on May 15, 2008. The defendants were expected to appeal it to the state supreme court.

14. The Milwaukee plan is the oldest surviving publicly funded voucher scheme. Several cities, however, including Washington DC, New York City, Baltimore, and Dayton, Ohio, have privately funded voucher plans. The most ambitious private efforts are through the Children's Scholarship Fund, which has already provided more than 62,000 "scholarships" (covering the period from 1999 to 2004).

15. In addition, prior to the federal constitutional challenge to the Cleveland law, the Ohio Supreme Court upheld the law against a challenge based on the state constitution's compelled support provision (*Simmons-Harris v. Goff*, 1999).

16. Kemerer (1998) reviewed each state's published legal decisions about Blaine provisions, and concluded that seventeen states would interpret their provision in a way that would be relatively restrictive: Alaska, California, Delaware, Florida, Hawaii, Idaho, Kansas, Kentucky, Massachusetts, Michigan, Missouri, North Dakota, Oklahoma, South Dakota, Virginia, Washington, and Wyoming (181–82). Puerto Rico (*Asociación de Maestros*, 1994) should be added to this list. He listed another 12 states that lean toward more permissive interpretations of their Blaine language: Alabama, Arizona, Maine, Maryland, Mississippi, Nebraska, New York, Pennsylvania, Rhode Island, South Carolina, Utah, and West Virginia (Kemerer, 1998, 181–82). To this permissive list, we can now add Wisconsin (*Jackson*, 1998), Illinois (*Toney*, 2001), and Ohio (*Simmons-Harris*, 1999), but the Arizona *Cain* (2008) decision should, for the time being at least, move it from the permissive to the restrictive list. According to Kemerer, 16 Blaine states remain uncertain: Arkansas, Colorado, Connecticut, Georgia, Indiana, Iowa, Louisiana, Minnesota, Montana, Nevada, New Hampshire, New Jersey, New Mexico, Oregon, Tennessee, and Texas.

17. Compelled-support language has a less controversial history than Blaine language, but these clauses, too, could be neutralized using the *Romer* approach. Moreover, compelled support clauses are less likely to require the invalidation of voucher legislation. See *Simmons-Harris* (Ohio, 1999). But see *Chittenden* (1999), where the Vermont Supreme Court held that statutes authorizing a tuition reimbursement scheme transgress the compelled support clause of the Vermont Constitution (Vt. Const. ch. I., art. 3).

18. Article I, §11 of the Washington Constitution provides, in part:

> Absolute freedom of conscience in all matters of religious sentiment, belief and worship, shall be guaranteed to every individual, and no one shall be molested or disturbed in person or property on account of religion; . . . No public money or property shall be appropriated for or applied to any religious worship, exercise or instruction, or the support of any religious establishment.

In addition, Article IX, §4 states, "All schools maintained and supported wholly or in part by the public funds shall be forever free from sectarian control or influence."

19. This law is currently being challenged in *Genier v. McNulty* (2003).

20. A challenge to the Maine law was rejected in *Bagley v. Raymond School Department* (1999). However, a new challenge was filed after *Zelman* was decided (*Anderson v. Town of Durham*, 2002).

21. Interestingly, had the *Davey* decision been affirmed by the Supreme Court, a state court faced with a statute including severability language would have to reject the invitation to sever a statute (allowing vouchers only for secular private schools), because to do so would yield a non-neutral policy. For example, Proposition 38, the voucher initiative on California's November 2000 ballot, contained a limited severability clause (section 8.8) providing that a court determination that vouchers cannot be redeemed at any particular class of schools (e.g., religious schools) would not prevent the vouchers from being redeemed at other schools (e.g., secular, private schools).

22. This is the same line of cases that provides the primary defense against challenges to the No Child Left Behind Act of 2001. States are free to decline federal education (Title I) funding and would thereby not need to comply with requirements concerning Adequate Yearly Progress, disaggregation of test score results, and so forth (Welner, 2005).

23. The relevant provision was instead Article I, §11 ("No public money or property shall be appropriated for or applied to any religious worship, exercise or instruction"). See *Locke* (2004), p. 723, n. 7: "Neither Davey nor amici have established a credible connection between the Blaine Amendment and Article I, §11."

6

Policy and Political Implications

EARLIER CHAPTERS OUTLINED FEATURES of neovouchers that differ from direct vouchers. With these differences in mind, this chapter examines three key implications for policy and politics. First, neovouchers may be more fiscally advantageous to the state than direct vouchers. Second, they may face reduced political obstacles. Third, relative to direct vouchers, neovouchers hand over substantial decision-making control to wealthier taxpayers. The first two features appear to give neovouchers a leg up on their older cousins. The third, however, raises a cautionary note for equity-minded choice supporters.

Fiscal Effects

Although neovoucher policies have not been subjected to much empirical research, one type of study has been fairly common: analyses of the likely fiscal impact of the policy (see Collins Center for Public Policy, 2002; Gottlob, 2004; Lindsay, 2004; Maranto, 2003). A basic argument put forward by supporters of voucher policies, whether direct vouchers or neovouchers, hinges on the idea that public expenditures can leverage private money. When a parent sends a child to private school using a voucher with a face value of less than the per public operating cost in public schools, then—all other things being equal—the government's cost is less than it would have been if the child had attended public school.

The fiscal argument in support of neovouchers where the tax credit is not 100 percent, such as those in Iowa, Rhode Island, and Pennsylvania, is enhanced because the voucher itself is supplemented by private funding. If a corporation donates $5,000 and takes only a 90 percent ($4,500) tax credit, then the effective result is a state expenditure of $4,500 (given in a tax credit to the company) being used to leverage a $500 contribution from the company. Now assume that Pennsylvania's public schools have, on average, a per pupil operating cost of $9,000, and assume also that the $5,000 corporate donation is passed along as a neovoucher to help fund the private school education of a child who would have otherwise (if she had not been given the voucher assistance) attended a public school. The private school has an annual tuition of $10,000. The child's family comes up with the remaining $5,000. So a government investment of $4,500 generates a contribution of $500 from the corporation and a contribution of $5,000 from the family. The government savings are calculated at $4,500 (the per pupil operating cost of $9,000 minus the tax credit of $4,500).

Whether these savings are possible depends on each state's law. The corporate and individual tax credit policies in Arizona and Georgia are all for 100 percent of the donation, as is Florida's corporate tax credit. Pennsylvania's corporate tax credit is for 90 percent of the donation if the corporation makes a two-year commitment (75 percent otherwise). Rhode Island's corporate tax credit mirrors Pennsylvania's. Iowa's individual tax credit is for 65 percent of the donation. So this argument that neovouchers can generate savings beyond those of direct vouchers does not apply to Arizona, Florida, or Georgia but it does apply to Pennsylvania, Rhode Island, and (particularly) Iowa.

But this simple calculation neglects the potential effects of other tax benefits for parental and corporate expenditures. An individual could use the federal Coverdell Education Savings Account (allowing for tax-free withdrawals of investment earnings) to mitigate out-of-pocket costs associated with the tuition balance beyond the voucher amount. A corporation would almost surely take a deduction for the contribution amount not reimbursed by the tax credit. Using the above example, a Pennsylvania corporation that took a 90 percent credit on its $5,000 donation would then treat the remaining 10 percent ($500) as a deductible charitable contribution, reducing taxable income by that amount.[1] Continuing with the above example, the governmental savings would accordingly not be the full $4,500—after taking into consideration Coverdell tax breaks and corporate tax deductions. The number would likely be closer to $4,000.

The above calculation also does not account for the fact that many students who receive neovouchers would have attended private school even if they were forced to pay for it on their own. If, for instance, half the voucher recipients in the hypothetical Pennsylvania example would still have attended private school, then the calculation—assuming 100 recipients total—might look like the following:

- $4,000[2] in governmental savings for each of the 50 students who would have attended public school, or a total of $200,000 in savings.
- $4,500 in government cost for each of the 50 students who would have attended private school, or a total of $225,000 in additional costs.

The resulting $25,000 loss in this illustration is based on a basketful of hypothetical numbers and assumptions—it is not meant to concretely describe any particular state's program. But the factors set forth in this hypothetical situation are very real. As a rule, savings will only be realized if a substantial number of the students receiving the vouchers would otherwise have attended public school.

The potential for neovoucher policies to save public funds can be summarized with the following formula:

$$X = (S^*N^*F) - (D^*P) - ([D - (D^*P)](.07) + [D - (D^*P)](.30)) - (N^*F)(C - [(D^*F) + T])(.35) + E$$

X represents the state's annual net cost or savings;

S represents the state's average per-pupil public spending;

N represents the total annual number of neovouchers distributed;

F represents the fraction of N who are switchers from public school to private school in response to the neovoucher availability;

D represents the total of all taxpayer donations;

P represents the fraction of these donations allowed as a tax credit;

C represents the weighted average cost of private schooling in the participating private schools;

T represents the weighted average of the tuition paid by parents or guardians to the participating private schools; and

E is a variable reflecting each school district's enrollment capacity. If the school district is overcrowded, then the public may experience cost savings since the vouchered students will mitigate the overcrowding and lessen the likelihood that the district will have to respond by, for instance, building new schools. If the school district is under-enrolled or has stable enrollment, then the loss of vouchered students may result in additional cost due, for instance, to loss of efficiencies of scale—meaning that E takes on a negative value.

Looking now at each term in the equation, "S*N*F" is the reduction in public spending due to students who switched from public to private school. "D*P" is the total cost of all credits given to taxpayers in the state. These are the two main terms, and many advocates of neovouchers will end the discussion at this point.

The other terms, however, are also potentially important. "[D – (D*P)](.07) + [D – (D*P)](.30)" represents the state tax deduction on the amount of the donation not eligible for a tax credit, assuming a state income tax rate of 7 percent, as well as the federal tax deduction, assuming a federal marginal income tax rate of 30 percent. Finally, "(N*F)(C – [(D*F) + T])(.35)" is the amount of deductions taken for charitable donations to the private schools, to subsidize the additional students enrolled in these private schools. This assumes average marginal tax rates (combined federal and state) of 35 percent, it assumes no overhead charges by the nonprofit, and it assumes that the private schools attended by these voucher students are in fact subsidized with charitable giving, as is typically the case with Catholic schools.

Broken down into its component parts, this term multiplies the number of switcher neovouchers by the average difference between total cost of private schooling received by these switchers and the total tuition, paid jointly through the neovouchers and by the parents or guardians of the students. This product represents the total charitable donations used to supplement the education of these switchers, and it is multiplied by the average marginal tax rate.

Clearly, the potential for a neovoucher policy to save or cost the public coffers will depend on a variety of factors. (The formula leaves out the additional tax expenditure due to the Coverdell accounts.) Yet because the average costs of public and private schooling are not susceptible to much governmental manipulation, the variables that a state's voucher policy can tinker with are largely limited to the value of the voucher, the eligibility rules for students, and (in the case of neovouchers) the percentage of the tax credit. For instance, Iowa's decision to provide only a 65 percent tax credit puts that state on better financial footing. Likewise, Cleveland's direct voucher plan, with a maximum voucher value of $3,450 as of 2008, puts the government in a better fiscal position than does Milwaukee's, with a 2008 maximum value of $6,501, assuming that the lower voucher amount does not result in a corresponding reduction in switchers from public to private. (The value of any given neovoucher is generally determined solely by the nonprofits that accept the donations and package them for distribution to students and families.) Eligibility rules can limit recipients to those who transfer from a public school, or the rules can give priority to such students. For instance, Ohio's new "educational choice scholarship pilot program" is targeted primarily at students enrolled in public schools deemed failing under the state testing system. Students currently attending nonpublic schools are not eligible to apply, nor are homeschooled students. Similarly, students are eligible under Arizona's new corporate neovoucher program or the Florida and Georgia neovoucher programs only if they are transferring from a public school (or are entering kindergarten or—in Florida—first grade).

Each of these types of provisions has the effect of mitigating the governmental cost of a voucher program, or perhaps even turning the program into a fiscal benefit for the government. In the absence of any such provisions, as is the case with the original Arizona's neovoucher policy (for individual donations), the results can be stark. According to calculations by Arizona's pro-voucher Goldwater Institute, the state suffered a net loss of between $13 and $18 million in 2002–2003 (Lukas, 2003). The authors surveyed private schools, asking how many of their voucher recipients had transferred from public schools as a result of receiving the voucher. The survey indicated that approximately 12 percent of the neovouchers went to transferring students.[3] They calculated the resulting savings to the state as only about $11 million, compared to costs of about $26 million. The authors nonetheless offered optimistic projections for the future, arguing as follows:

> It seems likely that most of the need among those already enrolled in private schools is being met. It is thus reasonable to expect that a greater portion of the next $1 million raised by school tuition organizations would be granted to transferring students. Therefore, as participation in the program increases, it is probable that program costs will decrease, and eventually the savings generated will outweigh the costs. (Lukas, 2003, 17)[4]

In the absence of new survey data, this sanguine view remains only speculation. In fact, the logic does not appear to hold up well to close examination, given that the average Arizona neovoucher is quite small—only $1,788 in 2007 (Arizona Department of Revenue, 2008)—and thus leaves considerable room for current private school attendees to have their schooling further subsidized. Moreover, Lukas herself notes that, "Although there is no publicly available data on tuition in Arizona private schools, it is possible that some schools have raised tuition as a result of the availability of scholarship money" (Lukas, 2003, 16). Basic market-demand principles suggest that this might indeed happen. With more potential customers able to afford private school, many of those schools would be able to charge more and retain full enrollment (see Huerta and d'Entremont, 2007, and studies cited therein). Looked at another way, families of students attending any given private school would have their tuition payments subsidized, meaning that the school could continue to expect X amount from the family and an additional Y amount in subsidized money. This might, in fact, lead to a cyclical feedback mechanism, with tuition increasing and resulting in a corresponding demand for greater neovoucher subsidies, which in turn would promote further tuition increases.

The other factor to consider here would be supply; the increased demand and increased level of available funding can be expected to increase the number of private schools and enrollment slots in existing schools. More generally, private school entrepreneurs can, in fact, be expected to respond to a variety of intended and unintended incentives, including the following:

1. overall supply of children (i.e., rural areas would be less attractive);
2. overcrowding at nearby public (and private) schools;
3. supply of students with access (transportation) to the facility;
4. supply of families (or corporations) with sufficient wealth to donate—to take advantage of the tuition tax credit;
5. supply of families with the financial means to afford the tuition payment above the voucher amount, plus other expenses associated with private school education;
6. supply of students likely to achieve high test scores on any standardized achievement test required by the neovoucher legislation;
7. supply of students who are less costly to educate;
8. supply of students whose interests, beliefs, and background are consistent with the school's mission; and
9. supply of students whose behavior is consistent with the school's curriculum and its pedagogical approach.

This list highlights the reality that some students and parents are much more attractive, from an educational and financial perspective, than others (Lubienski, 2005). Private schools need to compete. They cannot be weighed down with students who pay little, cost much, take away from other students' educational experience, and make the school look bad in published reports about students' academic success. Schools that fail to compete using selective criteria such as those in the above list will run a heightened risk of failure (bankruptcy or closure).[5] How all this plays out will likely vary from state to state and even from community to community.

Overall, the fiscal story for neovouchers is both nuanced and uncertain. Depending on how the policy is drawn up, it has the potential to be revenue neutral or to either save or cost the state money. Each such fiscal decision, however, also has implications for other voucher goals. Decreasing the voucher amount would result in greater savings per voucher, but it would also decrease the incentive effect on current public school families; they are more likely to switch if offered $4,000 than if offered $1,000. Decreasing the amount of the voucher would also undermine the goal of meaningfully assisting low-income families who might want to choose private schooling. A voucher of $4,000 would provide a family in poverty with considerable private school choices; a voucher of $1,000 generally would not. Huerta and d'Entremont (2007) examined the modest tax credits (for family expenses) that have existed in Minnesota and Iowa and found that "current tax credit programs do not appear to have led to an increase in private school enrollments. Their main function appears to be to provide tax relief to parents who have already enrolled or intend to enroll their child in a private school; these families are disproportionately middle-class and affluent taxpayers" (98–99).

Reducing the tax credit from 100 percent to 65 percent would also result in greater savings to the state, but substantially fewer taxpayers can be expected to donate. This might result in a smaller number of vouchers (or a smaller amount per voucher). Limiting voucher eligibility to "switchers" also undermines important goals and might even lead to inefficiencies and game-playing. Do policy makers really want families to send their children to public school for a year just so that they can be eligible for a voucher the following year? In any case, the kindergarten exception will undermine much of the effectiveness of these provisions, since it provides little more than a short-term damper on the law's long-term fiscal effects (see the analysis in Welner, 2004). Today's kindergarteners are tomorrow's high-schoolers.

The calculation of neovouchers' likely fiscal impact gets even more complicated when one considers the fact that private school tuition is often subsidized by additional charitable donations, as explored in the penultimate term of the earlier equation. For instance, a Catholic school might charge only $3,000 in tuition, but the actual cost might be closer to $7,000. Tax-deductible donations to the church help fill that gap. If a child in Arizona transfers from a public school to a school run by the Phoenix Archdiocese, using a $2,000 neovoucher, the immediate savings to the state would approximate the public school cost minus the $2,000 tax credit. But a complete calculation of these savings should reduce that amount by the cost of the additional tax deductions given to those who made the charitable donations to the church.

The switch rate from public to private would also likely depend on preexisting private school attendance rates. In a state like Utah, with a beginning rate of 2.8 percent (compared to 12 percent nationally), the pool of existing private school students who might use voucher money is much smaller and the probability of state savings is correspondingly higher (see Herzberg and Fawson, 2004).

Finally, the practical fiscal effects depend in part on whether a school district is overcrowded. In a district facing enrollment levels that might require the construction of new buildings, the marginal cost of each additional student is relatively high and the government realizes a practical savings when such additional children enroll in private schools. In districts with stable enrollment or under-enrollment, the marginal cost of each additional student is relatively low; the district might have to close schools as a result of the voucher policy and would, in any case, likely lose efficiencies of scale. This factor may weigh in favor of the school choice expansion in Arizona, for instance, where the school-age population has been consistently increasing. But it may weigh against expansion of school choice in West Virginia, where that population has been decreasing.

Political Advantages of Tax Credits

Several factors combine to suggest that neovouchers may face lesser political obstacles than direct vouchers. First, as explained in chapter 5, neovouchers appear to be better able to survive constitutional scrutiny. Second, as noted above, neovouchers have the potential for greater fiscal savings. Third, neovouchers have a supply side appeal as well as the appearance of lesser spending because foregone revenues are less concrete than expenditure line items. Fourth, neovouchers tend to be less regulated than direct vouchers, which appeals to the same, often Republican, legislators who generally propose these bills. Fifth, the neovoucher approach institutionalizes an advocacy constituency among those people and organizations that implement the distribution system. And, finally, in terms of issue framing, neovouchers suffer from only a fraction of the rhetorical stigma associated with direct vouchers.

Legal

Because neovoucher laws may, in some states, dodge the Blaine amendment bullet, they may face less daunting state constitutional scrutiny than direct vouchers. This translates into a political benefit. A comparable scenario played out in the wake of Florida's *Bush v. Holmes* (2006) decision finding the state's direct voucher law to be in violation of a provision in the state constitution requiring a uniform system of public education. (Although an earlier court had also found the voucher law to violate the state's Blaine amendment, the state's Supreme Court did not reach that issue. Republican leaders passed legislation to effectively continue the voucher program but fund it through an expansion of the state's corporate neovoucher policy (Klas, 2006). Supporters of neovouchers saw this legal advantage as crucial to future strategic planning: "Tax-credit programs [are] bulletproof. They have survived all legal challenges, and they fare better than vouchers in polls. They also put taxpayers in the driver's seat alongside parents" (Lamer, 2006). The two approaches are relatively interchangeable, so if direct vouchers suffer a court defeat, neovouchers can step in to fill the void with relative ease.

Fiscal

Tax credits may also have political advantages associated with fiscal concerns. Supporters of both direct and neovouchers generally argue that the policies will save states money, as described earlier in this chapter. So long as the grant is for substantially less than a state's per pupil student funding and the policy is designed to draw sufficient numbers of students from the public schools, the shifting of students from public to private schooling carries this potential for savings. This money-saving effect is reversed, however, for each voucher used by a student already enrolled in a private school (or who would have, even in the absence of the voucher policy, enrolled in a private school).

While this savings argument plays out equally for direct and neovouchers, two other fiscal arguments politically favor tuition tax credits. As already noted, tax credits can be designed to encourage taxpayers to contribute money beyond the amount credited, if the credit is for less than the full donation. The second potential advantage, however, is really more political than fiscal: in times of tight budgets, tax credits may simply *look* better than spending increases. It is true that when a legislature is tightening the state's belt, it is politically difficult to pass either a major tax credit or a major expenditure; to a large extent, fiscal crises undermine the political viability of both types of legislation. But many taxpayers perceive a tax credit as a tax cut, even though the practical budgetary effect is the same as a direct expenditure. Looking only at this issue of perception (additional practical differences are discussed below), tax credits may be easier to sell—particularly if they can be marketed as saving revenue or as revenue-neutral. In fact, state fiscal analysts, who summarize bills for legislators, may offer a more speculative summary of costs to the state, because foregone revenues are less concrete than expenditure line items.

Supply-Side Appeal

The practical (beyond perception) side of this distinction lies in the difference between Keynesian spending arguments and supply-side arguments. Is the economic stimulus greater if the government redistributes tax revenue through desired programs, or is it greater if the government cuts taxes and gives more spending (or saving) discretion to putative taxpayers? Depending on one's perspective, both vouchers and neovouchers may be sold as an economic stimulus, but the credit approach may carry an advantage—since (setting aside academic or empirical contentions) supply-side theories seem to have more political currency among the likely supporters of vouchers than do Keynesian spending arguments. Moreover, the key argument of the *Kotterman* (1999) court, viewing foregone taxes as something other than lost revenues, likely will appeal to legislators for political reasons in addition to legal reasons. The basic contention that potential tax money belongs to taxpayers, not to the government, rings just as true in tough economic times as it does in times of plenty.

A related political benefit is that, as opposed to direct vouchers, neovouchers require more active engagement with education on the part of private citizens. Primarily, this increased involvement is on the part of taxpayers who donate the money, as well as the citizens who form and run the nonprofit organizations that receive donations and distribute vouchers. Referring to the flow charts in chapter 2, one can see that the additional steps inserted into the neovoucher approach depend greatly on nongovernmental actors. This is not a coincidence, since the approach is designed in part to convince courts that intervening private decision-making insulates the neovoucher policies from constitutional challenges to state funding of religious institutions.

Governmental Regulation

Expenditures of state money usually come with regulatory strings attached. When asked about vouchers, Americans overwhelmingly favor requiring recipient schools to meet a variety of requirements such as state curriculum standards (88%) and the hiring of only certified teachers (86%) (Peter D. Hart Research Associates, 1998). But many or most private schools would not be willing to accept such conditions (Muraskin, 1998, 49, exh. 32). Testing, curriculum, and—in particular—admissions requirements are anathema to many private, religious schools (Omand, 2003). This tension suggests a political hurdle that some voucher plans may not be able to clear. In contrast, tax credit policies seem less likely to face such a challenge, given the additional distance between the governmental allocation and a school's receipt of money. On this basis, some conservatives have argued that neovouchers should be favored over direct vouchers (Lamer, 2006; Omand, 2003).[6]

Regulation, however, is still possible. In 2008, Iowa adopted a new curriculum mandate, setting forth basic skills and concepts, applicable to nonpublic schools receiving state accreditation (Robelen, 2008). Because such accreditation is a prerequisite for receipt of a neovoucher, this seems like precisely the sort of intervention feared by Omand, Lamer, and other free-market advocates. (The top Catholic school officials in the state, however, supported the measure, citing its "flexibility.") As this instance makes clear, a shift from vouchers to neovouchers does not offer blanket protection against increased regulation.

Institutionalized Constituency

Looking back to figure 2.1, which diagrams the differences between the neovoucher and traditional voucher approaches, one feature stands out: the creation of nonprofit corporations that receive and distribute taxpayer donations. These organizations, as well as their directors, officers, and employees, thus become an institutionalized advocacy constituency. They join recipient parents and private schools as potentially powerful beneficiaries of the neovoucher system, lobbying to maintain and expand the policy. These nonprofit corporations also assist in the success of the neovoucher system by helping to inform potential parents and taxpayers of the opportunities presented by the law—a role that would otherwise, in a traditional voucher system, be primarily played by advocacy groups and the government.

Issue Framing

Finally, and perhaps most importantly, is the political advantage grounded in the idea of issue framing (Lakoff, 2004). Opponents of vouchers have succeeded in framing the policy as, in significant part, an attack on public schools. One response to this negative framing of the term "vouchers" has been a renaming of vouchers as "opportunity scholarships." Republican political advisor Frank Luntz advocated this change, explaining that the latter term is more popular (Editors, 2004; Feldman, 1997; see also Tannen, 2003). Luntz wrote a guide called *Language of the 21st Century* in which he recommended this change (among others) and explained that two-thirds of the public prefer "opportunity scholarships," while fewer than 23 percent prefer "vouchers" (Feldman, 1997).[7] *Education Week* reporter Michele McNeil wrote recently that while "conservatives have given up on . . . the word 'vouchers' . . . [t]he idea of vouchers is still very much alive" (McNeil, 2008).

But a second, more comprehensive response to the negative image of vouchers is a restructuring of vouchers as tuition tax credits. In 2003, following the Supreme Court's Cleveland decision and with Republicans in control of the Colorado legislature and governor's office, the legislature considered both a voucher bill and a tuition tax credit (neovoucher) bill. The politics were such that either bill could pass, but the press coverage was nonetheless interesting. The voucher legislation labeled the payments as "opportunity scholarships," but this subterfuge had limited success—the press coverage overwhelmingly used the simpler and more understandable term "vouchers." In contrast, potential press coverage of the tuition tax credit bill (which also incorporated the "scholarships" language) had more than just this one linguistic obstacle to maneuver around. Tax law is rarely covered in a detailed way in mainstream news; it is generally seen as too intricate and arcane for average readers, listeners, or viewers. Because of this, the debate dynamics appeared to change, with proponents of neovouchers attempting to explain the proposal sufficiently *to convince people of its benefits,* while opponents attempted to explain it sufficiently *to make the connection to vouchers.* The added complexity of the tuition tax credit approach gives it greater insulation against close inspection from newspapers, radio, and television, with associated benefits and detriments to its political appeal. For instance, in Colorado in 2003, the voucher proposal received much more press attention than the tuition tax credit proposal, which remained (for most Colorado residents) incomprehensible and obscure throughout its short legislative life.[8]

Overall, the political benefits of neovouchers—which overlap with the legal and fiscal benefits—do seem to be greater than those of direct vouchers.[9] Perhaps this is why even Democratic governors in Arizona and Pennsylvania have been willing to expand neovoucher plans, albeit only in the context of compromises with Republican-dominated legislatures (Davenport, 2006; Murphy, 2007). But as discussed in the next section, neovouchers also come with some drawbacks in comparison to traditional vouchers.

Transferring Control over Spending

The neovoucher plans providing personal income tax credits, which exist in Arizona, Iowa, and Georgia, tend to favor wealthier residents—those who owe substantial taxes—while the corporate neovoucher plans (in Arizona, Florida, Georgia, Pennsylvania, and Rhode Island) delegate power to those people with decision-making authority for corporations. As a result, wealthier taxpayers have effective control over which schools—and to some extent, which families—receive the funding. Viewed in terms of effects, the practical distinction between direct vouchers and neovouchers is that the initial allocation decision for the former is through representative democracy and for the latter is through a caricature of direct democracy—with the wealthy entitled to more votes. That is, the tax credit mechanism results in the allocation of tax benefits to support those institutions that are most popular with the state's wealthiest residents.

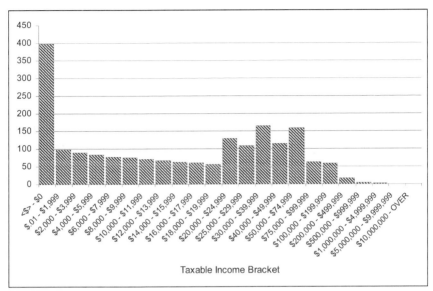

FIGURE 6.1
Average Number of Arizona Returns, 2000–2004 (in thousands)

This pattern is apparent from Arizona taxpayer data for the five-year period from 2000 to 2004. Figure 6.1 shows the distribution of taxpayers by income bracket. Each year, approximately 400,000 taxpayers have taxable income above $40,000, while approximately 1.5 million have taxable income below that threshold.

This distribution is important because taxpayers with incomes below $40,000 have a substantially lesser probability of itemizing their returns (figure 6.2). That likelihood begins to escalate sharply at higher income levels, such that more than 90 percent of taxpayers in the bracket from $75,000 to $99,999 itemize, as do 96 percent of taxpayers in the $100,000 to $199,999 bracket.

A married couple in Arizona that itemizes and owes $1,000 in state taxes can, of course, opt to pay these taxes into the state general fund. They can also opt to make charitable donations and reduce their taxes pursuant to the ordinary charitable deduction, or they could reduce their taxes by taking advantage of one of many tax credits in the state (e.g., homeowners can claim a 25 percent tax credit on up to $4,000 of solar devices installed on a residence [A.R.S. §§ 44-1761, et seq.]). But the neovoucher program offers the couple the unique option of essentially redirecting their $1,000 state tax obligation to a private school of their choice. In fact, as explained in chapter 4, the law has effectively allowed the couple to cooperate with another couple with children

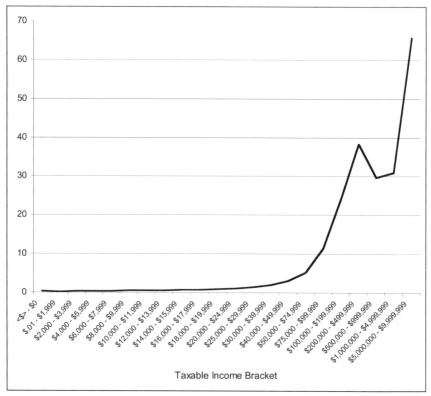

FIGURE 6.2
Odds of Itemizing, Arizona, 2000–2004

at a given private school, each directing their putative tax money to offset tuition owing for the other couple's child. Importantly, this mechanism for state support for the private schooling of a taxpayer's child is, for all practical purposes, available only to wealthier taxpayers; while a private school serving lower-income families might benefit from the Arizona neovoucher policy, its parent-taxpayers are much less likely to have substantial personal tax obligations that they could divert to (in effect) help their own children.

Glen Wilson's (2002) analysis of Arizona's public school tax credit (funding extracurricular activities) confirmed that who donates plays an important role in who receives. Looking at data from 1998 to 2000, Wilson found that the wealthiest 25 percent of public schools received 52 percent of the donated resources (a per-school mean of $20,500), while the poorest quarter of public schools received only 10 percent (a per-school mean of $3,900). The tax credit policy allows wealthy taxpayers to target the beneficiaries of their putative tax dollars, and it appears that they chose to help schools in their own neighborhoods. This should not be a surprise, nor are these condemnable choices for the individual taxpayers. But policy makers should be aware of the likely outcomes of such policies: extraordinarily regressive tax expenditures.

The means-testing provisions that other states with neovouchers have elected to incorporate into their policies undoubtedly help to mitigate these imbalanced outcomes. Even in Iowa, where neovoucher eligibility extends to families with incomes at 300 percent of the federal poverty level, the wealthiest families are screened out. That is, while they can donate and receive a tax credit, they cannot receive the voucher itself. One might expect to see stratified distributions among the eligible families—with those in the middle income range receiving more voucher money than those in the true poverty range—but means-testing provisions will prevent the extreme situations witnessed in Arizona.

The following, final chapter looks at such specific differences between various neovoucher policies and outlines a set of equity-focused recommendations. It also considers some troubling features of neovoucher policies—ones that cannot realistically be eliminated by well drafted legislation—and explores some difficult "slippery slope" issues around establishment clause concerns. The book concludes by relating tuition tax credits back to the broader choice discourse, discussing the democratic implications of these programs.

Notes

1. Pennsylvania's "REACH Foundation," a primary force behind the neovoucher law in that state, has presented computations that would allow at least some corporations to take the deduction using the full donation, without subtracting the amount of the credit, thus allowing the corporation to recoup all or almost all of the donation (REACH).

2. This is an approximation, taking into account the Coverdale and deduction adjustments.

3. Wilson (2002) focused on the proportionate distribution of money (rather than recipients) and calculated that 19 percent of the donated money in Arizona went to fund vouchers for transferring students (see also Belfield, 2001).

4. Lukas (2003) also adds the reasonable argument that some of the recipients may have been students enrolled in private schools who might have had to return to public schools for financial reasons but for the receipt of the voucher. She guesses that this applies to 10 percent of private school recipients, however, which seems quite high.

5. Of course, the universe of private schools includes some wonderful schools serving expensive and/or difficult student populations. Some of these schools are subsidized by churches and temples as part of their missions. Others are the projects of educational visionaries. In each case, these educational entrepreneurs are primarily

responding to incentives and disincentives other than those created by states' funding and accountability systems.

6. For an extensive discussion of the practical and regulatory benefits of neovouchers over traditional vouchers, written from a passionately free-market perspective, see Schaeffer (2007).

7. Luntz also suggested use of the term "parental choice" rather than "school choice" (Feldman, 1997).

8. Based on the author's analysis of Nexis search results, the two major Denver papers collectively ran two articles, one editorial, and one wire-service story on the tuition tax credit bill. During the same time period, these papers ran a combined 19 articles, seven editorials, and five wire-service stories on the voucher bill. The two proposals were initially thought to have approximately equal chances of passage, and both proposals passed through the state House. But after the state Senate passed the voucher proposal, the tax credit proposal never reached a final vote. The above tally is only through March 28, 2003, when the voucher bill was passed. That is, the tally does not include articles about the governor signing the bill or the subsequent legal challenges.

9. See the discussion of polling data in Schaeffer (2007).

7

Future Prospects

Tinkering with Utopia

TAX POLICY IS A VERSATILE TOOL. While some advocates of economic stimulus, for instance, may argue in favor of tax cuts for the rich, others may argue for cuts and credits for lower-income taxpayers. Both are tax cut approaches, and both are promoted as ways to improve the economy, but the policies are very different. Similar import attaches to the specifics of a neovoucher policy. Due to those specifics, the Arizona policy is very different from Florida's. In short, "the rules matter" (Arsen, Plank, and Sykes, 2000).

This chapter begins with an examination of some of the more important of those rules: means-testing, public-school switcher requirements, a public school element to the tax credit policy, the earmarking of donations, and whether the tax credit is for 100 percent of a donation. Policy variability is illustrated using the neovoucher plan proposed in Colorado in 2003. Although such design features can further particular goals, certain characteristics of neovouchers will always remain in place, including key drawbacks that policymakers should seriously consider before moving forward. Following a consideration of those issues, this final chapter examines "slippery slope" arguments in relation to establishment clause concerns, and it then concludes with a broader discussion of school choice and its democratic implications.

Designing an Equitable Policy

Consider the effects of differences between current neovoucher policies. Because Florida's neovoucher policy is means-tested, one would expect that the families benefiting from that policy have substantially greater financial need than do the recipients of Arizona's non-means-tested policy. Similarly, eligibility is more narrowly targeted by the Florida requirement that students beyond first grade have attended public school full time during the previous year. And one would expect that the Arizona problem of earmarked donations was avoided in Pennsylvania, where the practice is prohibited. Iowa's decision to limit its tax credit to only 65 percent of the donation also has important policy implications (for the state budget, for the charitability of the taxpayer action, and potentially for the program's size). These illustrate the sorts of decisions a legislator might make in crafting a neovoucher policy.

Several years ago, legislators in Colorado introduced a neovoucher bill including elements that provide a good starting point for a well-designed policy (HB03-1137; see also Welner, 2003):

1. The tax credit is valued at 50 percent of the donated amount;
2. The bill imposed a cap on the amount of each donation;
3. It imposed an overall ceiling on annual credits given, and it included a practical mechanism to help administer this ceiling;
4. A portion of all donated money must go to students switching from public to private schools;
5. From each tax-credited donation, 60 to 75 percent would go to help pay nonpublic school tuition; the remaining 25 to 40 percent would go to help students in public schools designated as "low" or "unsatisfactory" in the state's school accountability reports;[1]
6. An eligible student's household income must be within 200 percent of the federal poverty level;
7. For those students receiving funding as "public-to-private" (switchers), the neovoucher must be for at least 30 percent of the student's annual private school tuition; and
8. To be eligible to enroll students using the neovouchers, the private school must consent to administer annual tests to the recipient students (but, in the case this bill, not necessarily the state standardized test given to public school students).

The mechanism outlined by the Colorado legislation differed somewhat from the typical neovoucher approach. It adds a third step: the taxpayers' direct dealings are with a privately created, nonprofit corporation (the Designated Nonprofit Organization, or DNO), which then follows the taxpayers' directives in allocating this money to another nonprofit, which serves as the equivalent of Arizona's STO (these were called Certified Nonprofit Educational Assistance Organizations, or CNEAOs).

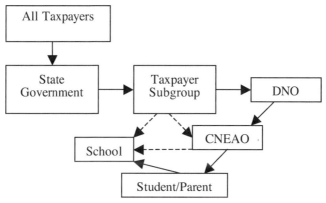

FIGURE 7.1
Colorado Proposal

Although each taxpayer's direct dealing under this proposed plan would be with the DNO, she or he (or it, since corporations would have been eligible) would be entitled to designate the CNEAO to which the DNO then distributes the money.[2] Moreover, because CNEAOs would have been likely to be affiliated with a given nonpublic school, the taxpayer could have effectively designated the school that ultimately would benefit from the donation. The dashed lines in figure 7.1 show this close relationship between the taxpayer, school, and CNEAO.

This Colorado legislation would have resulted in the government footing at least half the bill for the neovouchers, through directly foregone revenues.[3] But control over the funding would have been taken from the government and given to two other parties: (a) individual taxpayers, who would decide upon the CNEAOs (and thereby the schools) to which the funds would be allocated; and (b) individual CNEAOs, which would decide the grant recipient families and would effectively decide the recipient schools. These aspects of the legislation raise the same issues as were discussed for Arizona's law and the laws in the other neovoucher states.

But the Colorado legislation also demonstrates how concerns, particularly short-term equity concerns, are remediable through careful drafting. Using the above-described proposal as a jumping-off point, one could imagine an equity-minded and fiscally restrained neovoucher policy with the following characteristics:

- *A tiered means-testing provision, providing initial voucher funding for families at or below the federal poverty level and then providing remaining funding for families at or below 200 percent of poverty.* Cleveland's voucher policy takes a similar approach.

- *Students must attend public school full time during the year prior to receiving the voucher.* Part of the rationale for such a provision is fiscal; it ensures that all students are switchers.[4] Another feature is that it targets the benefit only at those families who are at least willing to try public schools. But this is also an element of unfairness. Why should, for example, those religious families that feel that they cannot consider public schools be in a worse position than other families who prefer nonpublic schools? Another drawback to such a provision is that students will attend public school for one year, thereby increasing transiency and associated disruptions, even though they would very much prefer private schooling (with associated problems of cost and of skewed decision-making).
- *No earmarking of donations to students, families, schools, or school-tuition organizations.* Policymakers may want to prevent earmarking to schools, but this can only realistically be accomplished by also preventing the designation of a given school-tuition organization (since the STO is generally associated with a given school or set of schools). Using the above Colorado proposal for this illustration, this proposed provision would require the taxpayer to donate to the DNO; the CNEAO role would be eliminated. The DNO would distribute the neovouchers to parents who would then make an unencumbered school-attendance decision. This aspect of the policy would mirror school voucher plans in places like Washington DC, Cleveland, and Milwaukee. Parents would take back some of their decision-making power from taxpayer-donors.[5]
- *Tax credit is for 50 percent.* Given marginal tax rates below 50 percent, this leaves intact the donation incentive to fund the neovouchers. But it also ensures that taxpayers are truly making charitable donations, rather than merely reallocating their tax obligations toward a preferred cause.
- *Each taxpayer has an annual tax credit cap.* For individuals, the tax credit should be no more than $2,000; for two individuals filing jointly, no more than $4,000; and for corporations, no more than $6,000. These cap amounts limit the disproportionate influence exercised by the wealthiest taxpayers.
- *The policy includes an overall tax credit ceiling.* Each state would have to determine the appropriate ceiling, based on perceived need and effects on the overall state budget.
- *One-third of donated money funds struggling public schools.* Voucher politics often have an us-against-them quality, with support and opposition arising out of one's values and beliefs about the enterprise of public schooling. Provisions like the one proposed here (or the one in Pennsylvania) curtail that dynamic. They provide support for needy families

wanting to pursue the private schooling option, but they simultaneously affirm support for the state's public schools.

- *Vouchers as full payment.* Private schools accepting students funded with neovouchers must accept the voucher amount as full payment for tuition. This provision would also effectively mean that the amount of each neovoucher is relatively high. The benefit of such a provision is that it protects struggling families from additional costs (beyond transportation and other associated expenses). The downside is that it reduces the number of vouchers made available and also would likely reduce the portion of private schools that would enroll vouchered students.
- *Testing and accountability.* Private schools accepting students funded with neovouchers must administer to vouchered students any assessments used for state accountability in public schools. This would allow for the program to be evaluated and allow for parental choices to be more informed. However, it would also place a burden on private schools and would interfere with their independence. And many or most private schools would not be willing to accept such conditions (Muraskin, 1998). The concession here that might make the provision palatable to private schools is that only the vouchered students would be tested, and that testing could be administered by local school district officials.
- *Anti-discrimination provisions.* Express anti-discrimination provisions should apply to the voucher-granting organizations as well as to any school accepting vouchered students. This raises difficult policy choices about discrimination categories. Certainly race and ethnicity should be covered, but what about sex, sexual orientation, English-language learner or special needs status, parental involvement, or prior measured ability? And what about religion?
- *The tax credit is refundable.* To increase donations and to more equitably distribute the option across taxpayers, the benefit should be structured as a refundable tax credit, with no itemization requirement. A refundable credit is one that allows low-income families to receive a tax refund from the state even if they owe no taxes, theoretically giving them the same economic benefits under the neovoucher policy as those in higher tax brackets. If the credit is for only 50 percent, one would not expect many lowest-income taxpayers to make these donations, but the option should nonetheless be available.[6]
- *Evaluation included.* Any neovoucher legislation should require data gathering and reporting regarding such matters as the family income and other demographics of recipients, the taxable income of the donors, the identity and nature of the recipient schools, the past school attendance

of the vouchered students, and key student outcomes. The evaluation
should also examine the effects of the policy on students in the public
schools from which vouchered students are leaving. And similar evaluation issues should be pursued with regard to the public school component of the law.

Together, these dozen elements would help frame a neovoucher policy with
considerable strengths. Each element also involves trade-offs and unintended
consequences, some of which are identified above. In pursuit of equity goals,
these elements also give short shrift to, and even stand in opposition to, the
ideal of choice for liberty's sake and the ideal of an unrestrained marketplace
(for an ardent defense of that marketplace approach, see Schaeffer, 2007).
Policy tradeoffs are inevitable under a voucher system just as they are under
a system of democratically governed public schools. But the specifics of an
ideologically motivated voucher system are unlikely to be shaped by the
sorts of empirical analyses that are the subject of this book. Accordingly, the
above elements are set forth for the benefit of policymakers who would look
to neovoucher policies as a practical way to assist needy families who would
otherwise have limited schooling options.

Drawbacks Notwithstanding Design

While specific provisions in particular tax credit laws may make them more
equitable, such fine-tuning nonetheless leaves in place a market-based framework, with its attendant strengths and weaknesses.

For instance, there is a policy tension facing supporters of voucher or
neovoucher policies targeted at lower-income families. On the one hand, they
assert that the programs save taxpayers money or are at least revenue neutral.
As discussed in chapter 6, this savings is achieved because, generally speaking,
the vouchers only supplement the private school tuition. Accordingly, when
a student leaves a public school and uses a voucher to attend a private school,
the cost of that student's education is no longer paid in full by the government. Instead, the government provides a partial subsidy, with the remainder
usually picked up by the child's family or by a private scholarship. Calculations showing governmental savings are generally based on models whereby
a limited number of students receive vouchers who would have attended
private schools anyway; for any such students, the state cost increases from
zero to the amount of the voucher. But this leads to a policy tension between
the desire to create a program that helps low-income families and one that is
(at least) revenue neutral. A program that shifts the cost of a child's educa-

tion from the government to that child's low-income family may benefit the family by providing more choice, but it does not leave the family in a better financial position.

Even assuming that the plan would yield a better education for participating students, is it proper for the state to accomplish this goal through a policy that requires low-income parents to pay, for instance, 30 to 50 percent of the education's cost? Why would a state want to move poor families from a system that covers the entire cost of their education into one in which only a half is covered?

One way to address or play down this tension is to argue that private education is simply more efficient and thus cheaper (Tierney, 2006). Alternatively, the suggestion above to design a neovoucher policy to give only a 50 percent tax credit offers another possible approach to avoiding or addressing the tension. Presumably wealthier donors, rather than low-income parents, provide the necessary supplement to the state's financial contribution.

The stratification that often occurs in market systems is another likely artifact of any voucher system. Current public school systems are themselves highly stratified, in fact, some advocates have suggested vouchers as a way to mitigate the educational segregation linked to housing segregation (Coons and Sugarman, 1978). But as discussed in chapter 2, evidence of the potential for such mitigation is far from encouraging. Consider one possible negative, but empirically grounded, scenario of what might happen in low-income urban areas.[7] One might anticipate a variety of schools arising to serve niche markets. Some of these would be church-affiliated, designed for parishioner families, and of varying quality. Others would range from high-quality, mission-oriented schools to those that might be described as "McSchools," providing low-cost education as an alternative to overcrowded and/or otherwise undesirable local public schools. Even though many of these would be average or lower-quality schools, they might appeal to a lower-income neighborhood's "elite" families—those with the most education, wealth, and involvement in their children's education and more likely to exercise active choice.

Overall, the effect of the policy would be to provide an alternative to a subpopulation skewed toward the best-behaved and highest-scoring students. Superficially, this may seem like an attractive scenario. Public schools in low-income urban areas would get some relief from overcrowding. And the neighborhood's families could exercise a choice that offers some students an improved (potentially, at least) set of educational opportunities. But consider the following drawbacks. First, because of logistical and parental efficacy limitations, only a subset of children in the poorest communities would likely have an opportunity to take advantage of the vouchers (Yettick, Love, and Anderson, 2008). Second, because of resource limitations and differential competitive pressures, most private school opportunities would likely still be well below those available in suburban private and public schools. Third, for these same financial reasons and because of the hypothetical business model designed to provide an oasis for select students, many of these private schools would (to the extent allowed) deny admission to the most costly and difficult students, such as students with disabilities. One of the hallmarks of private schools is that they, unlike most public schools, can select based on students' academic achievement, behavior, and parental involvement. Fourth, the overall impact of the legislation may be harmful. That is, even if the low-income urban students and families who move to private schools are found to benefit from the voucher policy, the entire population of these communities may suffer a detriment. Assuming that a substantial number of students shift from the public to the private schools, and assuming that the children and families that leave the public schools tend to be the wealthiest, best educated, and most involved (even within a means-tested subpopulation), then these already struggling public schools will be placed at a further disadvantage. That is, the policy could exacerbate, in those public schools, the problem of low achievement and its associated pathologies.

The suggestion above, that a third of all money donated be given to help struggling public schools, could be considered a form of "impact aid," designed to fund higher-quality educational opportunities for the students who remain. The success of such a provision, however, is uncertain.

One final point on the issue of school overcrowding, mentioned above. Recall the discussion in chapter 6 of overhead expenses, including the argument of neovoucher proponents to the effect that the legislation will result in a budget windfall. This anticipated windfall is grounded in part on the supposition that public schools will not suffer a loss in efficiency tied to overhead expenses, since the legislation will simply be alleviating overcrowding. Yet, as discussed above, the actual effects—*Which communities will see an increase in private school capacity? Which students within those communities will be provided with meaningful choices?*—are difficult to predict. Accordingly, many overcrowded schools may see no relief, and many schools at or below capacity may nonetheless lose students to private schools because of the tax credit program. As a means of addressing overcrowding, vouchers and neovouchers seem to be very blunt instruments.

Slippery Slope Concerns

As discussed in chapter 5, the establishment clause of the U.S. Constitution's First Amendment stood, for most of the twentieth century, as a solid barrier to voucher policies. That barrier was removed in 2002 by the Supreme Court's *Zelman* decision. Three years earlier, the Arizona Supreme Court's *Kotterman* (1999) decision gave voucher advocates a reason to hope that state constitutional provisions, similarly setting forth limitations on public support of religious institutions, could be circumvented by neovoucher policies. The majority in *Kotterman* reasoned that the funding never made its way into state coffers and could thus not be considered a public expenditure.

The following discussion begins with the *Kotterman* decision and asks what would realistically be left of the establishment clause if tax credits were not considered government allocations. The dissenting justices in *Kotterman* point out that the majority opinion's reasoning leaves no principled reason why the tax credit could not be increased far beyond $500, to pay the full cost of private, sectarian education. They attack the tax credit as "directed so that it supports only the specific educational institutions the Arizona Constitution prohibits the state from supporting—predominantly religious schools":

> By reimbursing its taxpayers on a dollar-for-dollar basis the state excuses them from paying part of their taxes, but only if the taxpayers send their money to schools that are private and predominantly religious, where the money may be used to support religious instruction and observance. If the state and federal religion clauses permit this, what will they prohibit? Evidently the court's answer is that nothing short of direct legislative appropriation for religious institutions is prohibited. If that answer stands, this state and every other will be able to use the taxing power to direct unrestricted aid to support religious instruction and observance, thus destroying any pretense of separation of church and state. (*Kotterman*, 1999, 645)

In fact, the rationale of the *Kotterman* majority would seem to open up many new avenues. To illustrate the change it could bring about, imagine first a law establishing the Gideons religious organization as the "Official Church of the U.S.A." Such a law would strike at the heart of the constitutional prohibition against laws "respecting an establishment of religion." Upon challenge, it would be declared unconstitutional. Now imagine a law providing government grants to religious organizations that provide reading materials for hotel rooms. This law, too, would quickly be seen as violating the establishment clause, because its principal or primary effect advances religion (*Lemon*, 1971, 612–13). Finally, imagine a law that provides a dollar-for-dollar tax credit to individuals who donate money to organizations that then grant the money to religious organizations that provide reading materials for hotel rooms. Although the Gideons would almost surely be the main beneficiary of this law, the reasoning of the majority in *Kotterman* would seem to allow this last law to withstand a constitutional challenge.[8]

A second aspect of the slippery slope concerns the concept of neutrality. The U.S. Supreme Court applied neutrality reasoning in its *Zelman* (2002) decision, and the Arizona Supreme Court grounds its *Kotterman* decision in such a neutrality argument. In a nutshell, basic education is compulsory for children in Arizona, but low-income parents had been coerced into accepting public education. These citizens had few choices and little control over the nature of their children's schooling because they could not afford a private education more compatible with their values and beliefs. Arizona's tax credit achieves a higher degree of parity by making private schools more accessible and providing alternatives to public education (*Kotterman*, 1999, 615). The court also noted that helping to pay for private school tuition helps to balance out the fact that the state already pays the cost of students' attendance at public schools. Chief Justice Rehnquist offered similar arguments in the *Zelman* (2002) case. Such rationales (i.e., such definitions of "neutrality") if carried to their logical conclusion would likely carry the nation toward the privatization ideals of Milton Friedman (1963, 1990). This could lead to nothing short of a revolution in American schooling.

Yet the most radical possibilities follow from the main *Kotterman* conclusion: that the tax credit mechanism circumvents the limitation on public spending—the court's rejection of the tax expenditure doctrine (see chapter 5). As the *Kotterman* dissent points out, if the majority's interpretation holds, then the government can use its taxing power (through tax credits) to direct unrestricted aid to support churches and other religious organizations. Direct taxpayer allocation of putative tax dollars could substitute for representative democracy. This might be done, for instance, using the positive check-off system presently included on federal 1040 forms to fund the Presidential Campaign Fund (see Welner, 2000, for an example of what this might look like). Could the rationale not be used to allow positive check-offs on state and federal taxes to fund any religious institution or activity? How about positive check-offs to fund the salaries of church ministers?

This may seem beyond the scope of possibility; the slippery slope argument can certainly be taken too far. But imagine someone in 1917 making a slippery slope argument about the War Revenue Act, which first allowed tax deductions for contributions to religious organizations. That person might have argued that such deductions would open the door to a complete discharge of tax obligations—to a 100 percent tax credit—in exchange for such a donation. In fact, this is very close to what we now see in Arizona and Georgia and (using slightly lesser percentages) the other four neovoucher states—the difference being that the donations go to an intermediary organization and then pass through the hands of parents before making their way to religious organizations. A parade of horrors may or may not occur, but the extensions beyond the current policies and laws require no major logical extensions of current legal doctrine.

Yet important checks do exist within the American system. Perhaps most importantly, a policy must clear political hurdles in addition to legal hurdles. Even after the Supreme Court announced that old-fashioned tax credits could be constitutional in 1983 and that vouchers could be constitutional in 2002, legislators in most states declined the invitations.

Moreover, the structure of the two religion clauses in the First Amendment creates a tension between free exercise and establishment that must, in many situations, be resolved by balancing the two interests. Recent decisions in the courts have cut back on establishment clause protections in favor of free exercise protections. But future decisions will not necessarily continue this trend. The Supreme Court may decide to hold the line, refusing to erode the establishment clause any further. Or it may shift back toward the strengthening of establishment clause protections. The key point here is that, given the inescapable tension between the free exercise clause and the establishment clause, even a logical extension of current legal arguments and current policies will not survive constitutional scrutiny unless the Court is willing to further trim away past establishment clause protections.

Choice and Democracy

Voucher policies, and school choice policies in general, advance an important form of liberty. Americans instinctively understand the value of parents exercising choice over key elements of their children's upbringing—including a child's school (see Galston, 1991). Yet Americans also understand that schooling is a public good; the education of a child serves the interests of the child, the child's parents, and the larger community and society (Oakes, Quartz, Ryan, and Lipton, 1999). Communities look to democratically elected school boards to give voice to the concerns of the larger public as well as individual parents. And it is not difficult for most Americans to see important distinctions between, on the one hand, a stratified marketplace for consumer items such as cars or laundry detergent and, on the other, a stratified marketplace for educational opportunities. Horace Mann's aspirational vision of schools as the "great equalizer of the conditions of men, [as] the balance wheel of the social machinery" (Mann, 1891 [1848], 251) is still an important part of the American narrative.

To date, no policies have aimed to replace public schools completely (or even overwhelmingly) with private ones.[9] Niche choice systems must expand considerably before they reach more than a relatively small subgroup of children. Accordingly, only policies that improve all public schools—where the majority of students (and the vast majority of impoverished students) will continue to be enrolled—have a direct, wide-ranging potential for upgrading the education of most children.

Moreover, the public, universal nature of schooling is implicated. Public schooling means more than publicly financed schooling.[10] In public schools, families are not asked to pay tuition, and students cannot be turned away because they are too poor, too difficult or expensive to educate, or of a disfavored religion. This last statement is surely controversial, and it is unfair to the many private schools that take all comers. (It is also too generous to those public schools that directly or indirectly erect barriers to true open admissions.) But there does exist a qualitative difference in the basic distributional imperatives of the two systems. Something is gained when we shift to a market-based distributional system, but something is also lost.

The inherent value of choice should also not be overstated. Schwartz (2004) points out that people given more choices are often less happy with whatever choice they make, even if it seems to be a good one. They wonder if a different choice might have produced even better results. Schwartz takes issue with the simplistic equating of choice with freedom:

> [M]ost Americans do not think that freedom is about exercising more and more choice. Even for those who do equate freedom with choice, having more choice does not seem to make them feel freer. Instead, Americans are increasingly bewildered—not liberated—by the sheer volume of choices they must make in a day. As behavioral scientists, we have found that the people who frame freedom in terms of choice are usually the ones who get to make a lot of choices—that is, middle- and upper-class white Americans. . . . The education, income and upbringing of these Americans grant them choices about how to live their lives and also encourage them to express their preferences and personalities through the choices they make. Most Americans, however, are not from the college-educated middle and upper classes. Working-class Americans often have fewer resources and experience greater uncertainty and insecurity. (Schwartz, Markus, and Snibbe, 2006, 14)

Of course, even choosers who seem more efficacious sometimes find choice to be troubling. Howe and his colleagues relate an anecdote from their study of the school choice system in Boulder, Colorado:

> [A] distraught parent called one day and asked, "Have I made a mistake? Should I be open-enrolling my daughter in . . . ?" She was worried about the wisdom of keeping her child in her assigned neighborhood school in light of the fact that its enrollment and test scores were dropping while its proportions of minorities,

students qualifying for free and reduced-price lunches, and students learning English as a second language were increasing. She was, by the way, a vociferous critic of the choice system. (Howe, Eisenhart, and Betebenner, 2001, 142)

Further, this issue of stratification by characteristics such as race implicates the democratic import of diverse interactions (see Macedo, 1991). A recent review of literature determined that diverse schooling tends to reduce prejudices (Tropp and Prenovost, 2008; see also Linn and Welner, 2007). School choice need not necessarily lead to greater overall segregation, but if policymakers are concerned about such unintended consequences, they should take care to include pertinent constraints in a policy's design. Moreover, as Justice Stevens pointed out, dissenting in the Cleveland voucher case, choice can lead to Balkanization—toward a separation by pre-existing preferences and traits and thus a loss of the American national and civic identity (*Zelman*, 2002; see also Barber, 1997).

A final democracy implication is unique to neovouchers, since these policies delegate, from elected state decision makers to taxpayers, a great deal of control over spending decisions. Effectively, this is an attack on the one-person, one-vote principle (*Baker v. Carr*, 1962), since wealthy taxpayers are much more likely to have an effectual vote in these spending decisions. Moreover, a gift backfilled by a 100 percent credit is not charity. When public disbursements are made other than through the elective system, representative democracy is sacrificed.

School Reform Implications

Voucher policies are most often promoted by highlighting problems in public schools, particularly inner-city schools serving low-income students of color (Chubb and Moe, 1990; *Zelman*, 2002). Most scholars who study American schooling, however, point to specific curricular and instructional reforms and interventions as most effective in helping such students—reforms such as early childhood education (Barnett, 2002; Reynolds, Temple, Robertson, and Mann, 2001), early reading intervention (Schwartz, Askew, and Gómez-Bellengé, 2007), class size reduction in grades K–3 (Finn, Gerber, Achilles, and Boyd-Zaharias, 2001; Krueger and Whitmore, 2002), and teacher quality (Allgood and Rice, 2002). The empirical research on vouchers has not shown the promise of these other reforms.

Yet, although vouchers are sometimes proposed as a comprehensive substitute for public education (most notably by Milton Friedman), many—probably most—voucher supporters see the two systems existing side by side. Accordingly, public school reform ideas such as those listed above should not be placed in a simplistic, false dichotomy with voucher reform. All too often, school reform discourse does seem to take on that either-or quality; if school dropout rates need to be addressed, for instance, should vouchers be the only solution (Gottlob, 2007)?

This is not to say that policymakers have an infinite capacity to juggle options, even if they are not in direct conflict. Moreover, personnel and other resources are limited. And meaningful reforms such as those outlined above generally do require a well-funded commitment. Vouchers can serve as a distraction—an easy answer—diverting attention (and concrete resources) away from proven solutions and real needs (akin to the "bread and circuses" of ancient Rome [Brantlinger, 1983]).

Similarly, vouchers can relieve the pressure to reform by giving a community's most efficacious parents an exit strategy. It is abhorrent to suggest that these parents should be trapped in unsuccessful schools just so that they can lobby for school improvement. But it is also abhorrent to design a system that consigns the majority of inner-city children to such unsuccessful schools and provides relief only to those children blessed with such efficacious parents. This is another false dichotomy; the choice for policymakers should never be between universal abandonment and an exit strategy for the few.

These dilemmas demonstrate that, while voucher reforms can exist side-by-side with reform efforts focused directly on improving public schools, neither type of reform effort can exist in a vacuum. Each affects the other, in terms of resources, efforts, attention, and in the many small ways that forces interact in a complex, open system (O'Day, 2002).

Conclusion

Neovouchers have managed to come a long way while flying under the voucher radar. As the current programs mature, policymakers will weigh new, experiential data as well as their own values, preferences, and beliefs concerning the relative benefits of private and public schooling. Like any meaningful educational policy, neovouchers come with both advantages and disadvantages, and they come with both intended and unintended effects.

I have personally come to appreciate these policies (and their underlying philosophies) as advancing a form of liberty. But I am also critical of the shift away from recognized practices of democratic control over education, and I am concerned that these policies appear to further stratify the educational experience. Perhaps most troubling for me is the possible abandonment of a key part of the civic mission of schooling, given the likely cycle of our current understandings of citizenship and democracy shaping our educational practices, and those practices then shaping our future understandings of these concepts. Wise policymakers will look down the road, experimenting with promising new approaches but always keeping in mind a long-term vision of American schooling and democracy.

Notes

1. The bill actually included an alternative for this remaining 25–40 percent, which would likely have diverted much of this money away from helping public schools (Welner, 2003). That alternative is not considered here.

2. A key part of the DNO's task was to cut off the allocation of credits after the annual limit is reached for a given year.

3. In addition to the 50 percent tax credit, the state and federal governments would likely have provided donors with a tax deduction for the remaining 50 percent.

4. Some policymakers might also want to require that the students' prior attendance be at an overcrowded school.

5. Based on an absolutist free-market rationale, earmarking has been defended by Schaeffer (2007, 29, fn. 58). Prohibiting earmarking for the benefit of one's own dependents, he wrote, "limits the freedom of taxpayers and families and the effectiveness of the program by eliminating personal relationships and interests from the program."

6. Note, however, that refundability of donations might undermine the legal argument of neovoucher advocates that state constitutional provisions are inapplicable because there exists no direct expenditure of public money.

7. While this scenario focuses on inner-city communities, it is also possible to speculate about other communities in response to a non-means-tested voucher policy. For instance, one might expect that elite private schools will grow or be built in some wealthier suburban communities, in response to overcrowding and to the added financial capacity provided by the state subsidy. One might also anticipate that in most rural areas transportation issues and overall lack of demand will result in no significant increase in private school supply.

8. For purposes of the federal establishment clause, this hypothetical hotel-reading-material law might be struck down because it does not necessarily serve a secular purpose and because it's difficult to characterize as merely an attempt to treat religious institutions in a neutral, accommodating way.

9. The distinction here is between unimplemented ideas and policy proposals with a reasonable chance of being adopted in the foreseeable future. Proposals for universal vouchers (Friedman, 1962) have certainly existed and have found a cohort of supports, and like-minded advocates are currently calling for a system of universal tuition tax credits (Lamer, 2006; Schaeffer, 2007). But no state has yet come close to such an expansive reform.

10. Compare this to the contention of Schaeffer (2007, 32): "All education providers—government, religious, or secular—constitute public education because all serve the public by educating children. Expanding the embrace of 'public' education is an overdue recognition of educational reality, not political semantics."

Appendix A

Arizona

Revised Statutes (A.R.S.) § 43 1089

§ 43-1089. Credit for contributions [by individual taxpayers] to school tuition organization
A. A credit is allowed against the taxes imposed by this title for the amount of voluntary cash contributions made by the taxpayer during the taxable year to a school tuition organization, but not exceeding:
   1. Five hundred dollars in any taxable year for a single individual or a head of household.
   2. Eight hundred twenty-five dollars in taxable year 2005 for a married couple filing a joint return.
   3. One thousand dollars in taxable year 2006 and any subsequent year for a married couple filing a joint return.
B. A husband and wife who file separate returns for a taxable year in which they could have filed a joint return may each claim only one-half of the tax credit that would have been allowed for a joint return.
C. If the allowable tax credit exceeds the taxes otherwise due under this title on the claimant's income, or if there are no taxes due under this title, the taxpayer may carry the amount of the claim not used to offset the taxes under this title forward for not more than five consecutive taxable years' income tax liability.
D. The credit allowed by this section is in lieu of any deduction pursuant to section 170 of the internal revenue code and taken for state tax purposes.

E. The tax credit is not allowed if the taxpayer designates the taxpayer's contribution to the school tuition organization for the direct benefit of any dependent of the taxpayer.

F. A school tuition organization that receives a voluntary cash contribution pursuant to subsection A shall report to the department, in a form prescribed by the department, by February 28 of each year the following information:

1. The name, address and contact name of the school tuition organization.
2. The total number of contributions received during the previous calendar year.
3. The total dollar amount of contributions received during the previous calendar year.
4. The total number of children awarded educational scholarships or tuition grants during the previous calendar year.
5. The total dollar amount of educational scholarships and tuition grants awarded during the previous calendar year.
6. For each school to which educational scholarships or tuition grants were awarded:
    (a) The name and address of the school.
    (b) The number of educational scholarships and tuition grants awarded during the previous calendar year.
    (c) The total dollar amount of educational scholarships and tuition grants awarded during the previous calendar year.

G. For the purposes of this section:

1. "Handicapped student" means a student who has any of the following conditions:
    (a) Hearing impairment.
    (b) Visual impairment.
    (c) Preschool moderate delay.
    (d) Preschool severe delay.
    (e) Preschool speech or language delay.
2. "Qualified school" means a nongovernmental primary school or secondary school or a preschool for handicapped students that is located in this state, that does not discriminate on the basis of race, color, handicap, familial status or national origin and that satisfies the requirements prescribed by law for private schools in this state on January 1, 1997.
3. "School tuition organization" means a charitable organization in this state that is exempt from federal taxation under section 501(c)(3) of the internal revenue code and that allocates at least

ninety per cent of its annual revenue for educational scholarships or tuition grants to children to allow them to attend any qualified school of their parents' choice. In addition, to qualify as a school tuition organization the charitable organization shall provide educational scholarships or tuition grants to students without limiting availability to only students of one school.

Arizona Revised Statutes (A.R.S.) § 43-1183

Credit for contributions [by corporate taxpayers] to school tuition organization

A. Beginning from and after June 30, 2006 through June 30, 2011, a credit is allowed against the taxes imposed by this title for the amount of voluntary cash contributions made by the taxpayer during the taxable year to a school tuition organization.

B. The amount of the credit is the total amount of the taxpayer's contributions for the taxable year under subsection A of this section and is preapproved by the department pursuant to subsection D of this section.

C. The department:
   1. Shall not allow tax credits under this section that exceed in the aggregate, a combined total of ten million dollars in any fiscal year.
   2. Shall preapprove tax credits subject to subsection D of this section.
   3. Shall allow the tax credits on a first come, first served basis.

D. For the purposes of subsection C, paragraph 2 of this section, before making a contribution to a school tuition organization, the taxpayer shall notify the school tuition organization of the total amount of contributions that the taxpayer intends to make to the school tuition organization. Before accepting the contribution, the school tuition organization shall request preapproval from the department for the taxpayer's intended contribution amount. The department shall preapprove or deny the requested amount within twenty days after receiving the request from the school tuition organization. If the department preapproves the request, the school tuition organization shall immediately notify the taxpayer that the requested amount was preapproved by the department. In order to receive a tax credit under this subsection, the taxpayer shall make the contribution to the school tuition organization within ten days after receiving notice from the school tuition organization that the requested amount was preapproved. If the school tuition organization does not receive the preapproved contribution from the taxpayer within the required ten days, the school tuition organization shall immediately notify the department and the department shall no longer include this preapproved contribution amount when calculating the limit prescribed in subsection C, paragraph 1 of this section.

E. A school tuition organization that receives contributions under this section shall allow the department to verify that the educational scholarships and tuition grants that are issued pursuant to this section are awarded to students who attend a qualified school.

F. If the allowable tax credit exceeds the taxes otherwise due under this title on the claimant's income, or if there are no taxes due under this title, the taxpayer may carry the amount of the claim not used to offset the taxes under this title forward for not more than five consecutive taxable years' income tax liability.

G. Co-owners of a business, including corporate partners in a partnership, may each claim only the pro rata share of the credit allowed under this section based on the ownership interest. The total of the credits allowed all such owners may not exceed the amount that would have been allowed a sole owner.

H. The credit allowed by this section is in lieu of any deduction pursuant to section 170 of the internal revenue code and taken for state tax purposes.

I. The tax credit is not allowed if the taxpayer designates the taxpayer's contribution to the school tuition organization for the direct benefit of any specific student.

J. A school tuition organization that receives contributions under this section shall use at least ninety per cent of those contributions to provide educational scholarships or tuition grants only to children whose family income does not exceed one hundred eighty-five per cent of the income limit required to qualify a child for reduced price lunches under the national school lunch and child nutrition acts (42 United States Code sections 1751 through 1785) and who either:

1. Attended a governmental primary or secondary school as a full-time student as defined in section 15-901 for at least the first one hundred days of the prior fiscal year and transferred from a governmental primary or secondary school to a qualified school.

2. Enroll in a qualified school in a kindergarten program.

3. Received an educational scholarship or tuition grant under paragraph 1 or 2 of this subsection if the children continue to attend a qualified school in a subsequent year.

K. In 2006, a school tuition organization shall not issue an educational scholarship or a tuition grant in an amount that exceeds four thousand two hundred dollars for students in a kindergarten program or grades one through eight or five thousand five hundred dollars for students in grades nine through twelve. In each year after 2006, the limitation amount for a scholarship or a grant under this subsection shall be increased by one hundred dollars.

L. A child is still eligible to receive an educational scholarship or tuition grant under subsection J of this section if the child meets the criteria to receive a reduced price lunch but does not actually claim that benefit.

M. The school tuition organization shall require that the children use the educational scholarships or tuition grants on a full-time basis. If a child leaves the qualified school before completing an entire school year, the qualified school shall refund a prorated amount of the educational scholarship or tuition grant to the school tuition organization that issued the educational scholarship or tuition grant to the child. Any refunds received by the school tuition organization under this subsection shall be allocated for educational scholarships or tuition grants to qualified children in the following year.

N. Children who receive educational scholarships or tuition grants under this section shall be allowed to attend any qualified school of their parents' choice.

O. A school tuition organization that receives a voluntary cash contribution pursuant to subsection A of this section shall report to the department, in a form prescribed by the department, by June 30 of each year the following information:

1. The name, address and contact name of the school tuition organization.

2. The total number of contributions received during the previous calendar year.

3. The total dollar amount of contributions received during the previous calendar year.

4. The total number of children awarded educational scholarships or tuition grants during the previous calendar year.

5. The total dollar amount of educational scholarships and tuition grants awarded during the previous calendar year.

6. For each school to which educational scholarships or tuition grants were awarded:

    (a) The name and address of the school.

    (b) The number of educational scholarships and tuition grants awarded during the previous calendar year.

    (c) The total dollar amount of educational scholarships and tuition grants awarded during the previous calendar year.

7. Verification that an independent review of financial statements according to generally accepted accounting principles was completed by a certified public accountant for the previous calendar year.

P. The department shall adopt rules necessary for the administration of this section.

Q. For the purposes of this section:

1. "Qualified school" means a nongovernmental primary school or secondary school:

   (a) That is located in this state, that does not discriminate on the basis of race, color, handicap, familial status or national origin and that satisfies the requirements prescribed by law for private schools in this state on January 1, 2005.

   (b) That annually administers and makes available to the public the aggregate test scores of its students on a nationally standardized norm-referenced achievement test, preferably the Arizona instrument to measure standards test administered pursuant to section 15-741.

   (c) That requires all teaching staff and any personnel that have unsupervised contact with students to be fingerprinted.

2. "School tuition organization" means a charitable organization in this state that both:

   (a) Is exempt from federal taxation under section 501(c)(3) of the internal revenue code and that allocates ninety per cent of its annual revenue for educational scholarships or tuition grants to children to allow them to attend any qualified school of their parents' choice.

   (b) Provides educational scholarships or tuition grants to students without limiting availability to only students of one school.

Appendix B

Florida

Title 14, Florida Statutes (Fla. Stat.) §220.187*

Credits for contributions to nonprofit scholarship-funding organizations
(1) FINDINGS AND PURPOSE.—
    (a) The Legislature finds that:
        1. It has the inherent power to determine subjects of taxation for general or particular public purposes.
        2. Expanding educational opportunities and improving the quality of educational services within the state are valid public purposes that the Legislature may promote using its sovereign power to determine subjects of taxation and exemptions from taxation.
        3. Ensuring that all parents, regardless of means, may exercise and enjoy their basic right to educate their children may promote using its sovereign power to determine subjects of taxation and exemptions from taxation.
        4. Expanding educational opportunities and the healthy competition they promote are critical to improving the quality of education in the state and to ensuring that all children receive the high-quality education to which they are entitled.
    (b) The purpose of this section is to:
        1. Enable taxpayers to make private, voluntary contributions to nonprofit scholarship-funding organizations in order to promote the general welfare.

---

* As amended in 2008.

2. Provide taxpayers who wish to help parents with limited resources exercise their basic right to educate their children as they see fit with a means to do so.
3. Promote the general welfare by expanding educational opportunities for children of families that have limited financial resources.
4. Enable children in this state to achieve a greater level of excellence in their education.
5. Improve the quality of education in this state, both by expanding educational opportunities for children and by creating incentives for schools to achieve excellence.

(2) DEFINITIONS.—As used in this section, the term:

(a) "Department" means the Department of Revenue.

(b) "Eligible contribution" means a monetary contribution from a taxpayer, subject to the restrictions provided in this section, to an eligible nonprofit scholarship-funding organization. The taxpayer making the contribution may not designate a specific child as the beneficiary of the contribution.

(c) "Eligible nonprofit scholarship-funding organization" means a charitable organization that:

1. Is exempt from federal income tax pursuant to s. 501(c)(3) of the Internal Revenue Code;
2. Is a Florida entity formed under chapter 607, chapter 608, or chapter 617 and whose principal office is located in the state; and
3. Complies with the provisions of subsection (6).

(a) "Eligible private school" means a private school, as defined in s. 1002.01(2), located in Florida which offers an education to students in any grades K-12 and that meets the requirements in subsection (8).

(b) "Owner or operator" includes:

1. An owner, president, officer, or director of an eligible nonprofit scholarship-funding organization or a person with equivalent decisionmaking authority over an eligible nonprofit scholarship-funding organization.
2. An owner, operator, superintendent, or principal of an eligible private school or a person with equivalent decisionmaking authority over an eligible private school.

(3) PROGRAM; SCHOLARSHIP ELIGIBILITY.—The Corporate Income Tax Credit Scholarship Program is established. A student is eligible for a corporate income tax credit scholarship if the student qualifies for free

or reduced-price school lunches under the National School Lunch Act and:

(a) Was counted as a full-time equivalent student during the previous state fiscal year for purposes of state per-student funding;

(b) Received a scholarship from an eligible nonprofit scholarship-funding organization or from the State of Florida during the previous school year;

(c) Is eligible to enter kindergarten or first grade; or

(d) Is currently placed, or during the previous state fiscal year was placed, in foster care as defined in s. 39.01.

Contingent upon available funds, a student may continue in the scholarship program as long as the student's household income level does not exceed 200 percent of the federal poverty level. A sibling of a student who is continuing in the program and resides in the same household as the student shall also be eligible as a first-time corporate income tax credit scholarship recipient as long as the student's and sibling's household income level does not exceed 200 percent of the federal poverty level. Household income for purposes of a student who is currently in foster care as defined in s. 39.01 shall consist only of the income that may be considered in determining whether he or she qualifies for free or reduced-price school lunches under the National School Lunch Act.

(4) SCHOLARSHIP PROHIBITIONS.—A student is not eligible for a scholarship while he or she is:

(a) Enrolled in a school operating for the purpose of providing educational services to youth in Department of Juvenile Justice commitment programs;

(b) Receiving a scholarship from another eligible nonprofit scholarship-funding organization under this section;

(c) Receiving an educational scholarship pursuant to chapter 1002;

(d) Participating in a home education program as defined in s. 1002.01(1);

(e) Participating in a private tutoring program pursuant to s. 1002.43;

(f) Participating in a virtual school, correspondence school, or distance learning program that receives state funding pursuant to the student's participation unless the participation is limited to no more than two courses per school year; or

(g) Enrolled in the Florida School for the Deaf and the Blind.

(5) AUTHORIZATION TO GRANT SCHOLARSHIP FUNDING TAX CREDITS; LIMITATIONS ON INDIVIDUAL AND TOTAL CREDITS.—

(a) There is allowed a credit of 100 percent of an eligible contribution against any tax due for a taxable year under this chapter. However, such a credit may not exceed 75 percent of the tax due under this chapter for the taxable year, after the application of any other allowable credits by the taxpayer. The credit granted by this section shall be reduced by the difference between the amount of federal corporate income tax taking into account the credit granted by this section and the amount of federal corporate income tax without application of the credit granted by this section.

(b) The total amount of tax credits and carryforward of tax credits which may be granted each state fiscal year under this section is:

1. Through June 30, 2008, $88 million.

2. Beginning July 1, 2008, and thereafter, $118 million.

(c) A taxpayer who files a Florida consolidated return as a member of an affiliated group pursuant to s. 220.131(1) may be allowed the credit on a consolidated return basis; however, the total credit taken by the affiliated group is subject to the limitation established under paragraph (a).

(d) Effective for tax years beginning January 1, 2006, a taxpayer may rescind all or part of its allocated tax credit under this section. The amount rescinded shall become available for purposes of the cap for that state fiscal year under this section to an eligible taxpayer as approved by the department if the taxpayer receives notice from the department that the rescindment has been accepted by the department and the taxpayer has not previously rescinded any or all of its tax credit allocation under this section more than once in the previous 3 tax years. Any amount rescinded under this paragraph shall become available to an eligible taxpayer on a first-come, first-served basis based on tax credit applications received after the date the rescindment is accepted by the department.

(6) OBLIGATIONS OF ELIGIBLE NONPROFIT SCHOLARSHIP-FUNDING ORGANIZATIONS.—An eligible nonprofit scholarship-funding organization:

(a) Must comply with the antidiscrimination provisions of 42 U.S.C. s. 2000d.

(b) Must comply with the following background check requirements:

1. All owners and operators as defined in subparagraph (2)(e)1. are, upon employment or engagement to provide services, subject to level 2 background screening as provided under chapter 435. The fingerprints for the background screening must be electronically submitted to the Department of Law Enforce-

ment and can be taken by an authorized law enforcement agency or by an employee of the eligible nonprofit scholarship-funding organization or a private company who is trained to take fingerprints. However, the complete set of fingerprints of an owner or operator may not be taken by the owner or operator. The results of the state and national criminal history check shall be provided to the Department of Education for screening under chapter 435. The cost of the background screening may be borne by the eligible nonprofit scholarship-funding organization or the owner or operator.

2. Every 5 years following employment or engagement to provide services or association with an eligible nonprofit scholarship-funding organization, each owner or operator must meet level 2 screening standards as described in s. 435.04, at which time the nonprofit scholarship-funding organization shall request the Department of Law Enforcement to forward the fingerprints to the Federal Bureau of Investigation for level 2 screening. If the fingerprints of an owner or operator are not retained by the Department of Law Enforcement under subparagraph 3., the owner or operator must electronically file a complete set of fingerprints with the Department of Law Enforcement. Upon submission of fingerprints for this purpose, the eligible nonprofit scholarship-funding organization shall request that the Department of Law Enforcement forward the fingerprints to the Federal Bureau of Investigation for level screening, and the fingerprints shall be retained by the Department of Law Enforcement under subparagraph 3.

3. Beginning July 1, 2007, all fingerprints submitted to the Department of Law Enforcement as required by this paragraph must be retained by the Department of Law Enforcement in a manner approved by rule and entered in the statewide automated fingerprint identification system authorized by s. 943.05(2)(b). The fingerprints must thereafter be available for all purposes and uses authorized for arrest fingerprint cards entered in the statewide automated fingerprint identification system pursuant to s. 943.051.

4. Beginning July 1, 2007, the Department of Law Enforcement shall search all arrest fingerprint cards received under s. 943.051 against the fingerprints retained in the statewide automated fingerprint identification system under subparagraph 3. Any arrest record that is identified with an owner's or

operator's fingerprints must be reported to the Department of Education. The Department of Education shall participate in this search process by paying an annual fee to the Department of Law Enforcement and by informing the Department of Law Enforcement of any change in the employment, engagement, or association status of the owners or operators whose fingerprints are retained under subparagraph 3. The Department of Law Enforcement shall adopt a rule setting the amount of the annual fee to be imposed upon the Department of Education for performing these services and establishing the procedures for the retention of owner and operator fingerprints and the dissemination of search results. The fee may be borne by the owner or operator of the nonprofit scholarship-funding organization.

5. A nonprofit scholarship-funding organization whose owner or operator fails the level 2 background screening shall not be eligible to provide scholarships under this section.

6. A nonprofit scholarship-funding organization whose owner or operator in the last 7 years has filed for personal bankruptcy or corporate bankruptcy in a corporation of which he or she owned more than 20 percent shall not be eligible to provide scholarships under this section.

(c) Must not have an owner or operator who owns or operates an eligible private school that is participating in the scholarship program.

(d) Must provide scholarships, from eligible contributions, to eligible students for the cost of:

1. Tuition and fees for an eligible private school; or

2. Transportation to a Florida public school that is located outside the district in which the student resides or to a lab school as defined in s. 1002.32.

(e) Must give priority to eligible students who received a scholarship from an eligible nonprofit scholarship-funding organization or from the State of Florida during the previous school year.

(f) Must provide a scholarship to an eligible student on a first-come, first-served basis unless the student qualifies for priority pursuant to paragraph (e).

(g) May not restrict or reserve scholarships for use at a particular private school or provide scholarships to a child of an owner or operator.

(h) Must allow an eligible student to attend any eligible private school and must allow a parent to transfer a scholarship during a school year to any other eligible private school of the parent's choice.

(i) 1. May use up to 3 percent of eligible contributions received during the state fiscal year in which such contributions are collected for administrative expenses if the organization has operated under this section for at least 3 state fiscal years and did not have any negative financial findings in its most recent audit under paragraph (l). Such administrative expenses must be reasonable and necessary for the organization's management and distribution of eligible contributions under this section. No more than one-third of the funds authorized for administrative expenses under this subparagraph may be used for expenses related to the recruitment of contributions from corporate taxpayers.

2. Must expend for annual or partial-year scholarships an amount equal to or greater than 75 percent of the net eligible contributions remaining after administrative expenses during the state fiscal year in which such contributions are collected. No more than 25 percent of such net eligible contributions may be carried forward to the following state fiscal year. Any amounts carried forward shall be expended for annual or partial-year scholarships in the following state fiscal year. Net eligible contributions remaining on June 30 of each year that are in excess of the 25 percent that may be carried forward shall be returned to the State Treasury for deposit in the General Revenue Fund.

3. Must, before granting a scholarship for an academic year, document each scholarship student's eligibility for that academic year. A scholarship-funding organization may not grant multi-year scholarships in one approval process.

(j) Must maintain separate accounts for scholarship funds and operating funds.

(k) With the prior approval of the Department of Education, may transfer funds to another eligible nonprofit scholarship-funding organization if additional funds are required to meet scholarship demand at the receiving nonprofit scholarship-funding organization. A transfer shall be limited to the greater of $500,000 or 20 percent of the total contributions received by the nonprofit scholarship-funding organization making the transfer. All transferred funds must be deposited by the receiving nonprofit scholarship-funding organization into its scholarship accounts. All transferred amounts received by any nonprofit scholarship-funding organization must be separately disclosed in the annual financial and compliance audit required in this section.

(l) Must provide to the Auditor General and the Department of Education an annual financial and compliance audit of its accounts and records conducted by an independent certified public accountant and in accordance with rules adopted by the Auditor General. The audit must be conducted in compliance with generally accepted auditing standards and must include a report on financial statements presented in accordance with generally accepted accounting principles set forth by the American Institute of Certified Public Accountants for not-for-profit organizations and a determination of compliance with the statutory eligibility and expenditure requirements set forth in this section. Audits must be provided to the Auditor General and the Department of Education within 180 days after completion of the eligible nonprofit scholarship-funding organization's fiscal year.

(m) Must prepare and submit quarterly reports to the Department of Education pursuant to paragraph (9)(m). In addition, an eligible nonprofit scholarship-funding organization must submit in a timely manner any information requested by the Department of Education relating to the scholarship program.

Any and all information and documentation provided to the Department of Education and the Auditor General relating to the identity of a taxpayer that provides an eligible contribution under this section shall remain confidential at all times in accordance with s. 213.053.

(7) PARENT AND STUDENT RESPONSIBILITIES FOR PROGRAM PARTICIPATION.—

(a) The parent must select an eligible private school and apply for the admission of his or her child.

(b) The parent must inform the child's school district when the parent withdraws his or her child to attend an eligible private school.

(c) Any student participating in the scholarship program must remain in attendance throughout the school year unless excused by the school for illness or other good cause.

(d) Each parent and each student has an obligation to the private school to comply with the private school's published policies.

(e) The parent shall ensure that the student participating in the scholarship program takes the norm-referenced assessment offered by the private school. The parent may also choose to have the student participate in the statewide assessments pursuant to s. 1008.22. If the parent requests that the student participating in the scholarship program take statewide assessments pursuant to s. 1008.22, the parent is responsible for transporting the student to the assessment site designated by the school district.

(f) Upon receipt of a scholarship warrant from the eligible nonprofit scholarship-funding organization, the parent to whom the warrant is made must restrictively endorse the warrant to the private school for deposit into the account of the private school. The parent may not designate any entity or individual associated with the participating private school as the parent's attorney in fact to endorse a scholarship warrant. A participant who fails to comply with this paragraph forfeits the scholarship.

(8) PRIVATE SCHOOL ELIGIBILITY AND OBLIGATIONS.—An eligible private school may be sectarian or nonsectarian and must:

(a) Comply with all requirements for private schools participating in state school choice scholarship programs pursuant to s. 1002.421.

(b) Provide to the eligible nonprofit scholarship-funding organization, upon request, all documentation required for the student's participation, including the private school's and student's fee schedules.

(c) Be academically accountable to the parent for meeting the educational needs of the student by:

1. At a minimum, annually providing to the parent a written explanation of the student's progress.

2. Annually administering or making provision for students participating in the scholarship program to take one of the nationally norm-referenced tests identified by the Department of Education. Students with disabilities for whom standardized testing is not appropriate are exempt from this requirement. A participating private school must report a student's scores to the parent and to the independent research organization selected by the Department of Education as described in paragraph (9)(j).

3. Cooperating with the scholarship student whose parent chooses to have the student participate in the statewide assessments pursuant to s. 1008.22.

(d) Employ or contract with teachers who have regular and direct contact with each student receiving a scholarship under this section at the school's physical location.

The inability of a private school to meet the requirements of this subsection shall constitute a basis for the ineligibility of the private school to participate in the scholarship program as determined by the Department of Education.

(9) DEPARTMENT OF EDUCATION OBLIGATIONS.—The Department
     of Education shall:
     (a) Annually submit to the department, by March 15, a list of eligible
          nonprofit scholarship-funding organizations that meet the re-
          quirements of paragraph (2)(c).
     (b) Annually verify the eligibility of nonprofit scholarship-funding
          organizations that meet the requirements of paragraph (2)(c).
     (c) Annually verify the eligibility of private schools that meet the re-
          quirements of subsection (8).
     (d) Annually verify the eligibility of expenditures as provided in para-
          graph (6)(d) using the audit required by paragraph (6)(l).
     (e) Establish a toll-free hotline that provides parents and private
          schools with information on participation in the scholarship pro-
          gram.
     (f) Establish a process by which individuals may notify the Depart-
          ment of Education of any violation by a parent, private school, or
          school district of state laws relating to program participation. The
          Department of Education shall conduct an inquiry of any written
          complaint of a violation of this section, or make a referral to the
          appropriate agency for an investigation, if the complaint is signed
          by the complainant and is legally sufficient. A complaint is legally
          sufficient if it contains ultimate facts that show that a violation of
          this section or any rule adopted by the State Board of Education has
          occurred. In order to determine legal sufficiency, the Department
          of Education may require supporting information or documenta-
          tion from the complainant. A department inquiry is not subject to
          the requirements of chapter 120.
     (g) Require an annual, notarized, sworn compliance statement by par-
          ticipating private schools certifying compliance with state laws and
          shall retain such records.
     (h) Cross-check the list of participating scholarship students with the
          public school enrollment lists to avoid duplication.
     (i) In accordance with State Board of Education rule, identify and
          select the nationally norm-referenced tests that are comparable to
          the norm-referenced provisions of the Florida Comprehensive As-
          sessment Test (FCAT) provided that the FCAT may be one of the
          tests selected. However, the Department of Education may approve
          the use of an additional assessment by the school if the assessment
          meets industry standards of quality and comparability.
     (j) Select an independent research organization, which may be a pub-
          lic or private entity or university, to which participating private

schools must report the scores of participating students on the nationally norm-referenced tests administered by the private school. The independent research organization must annually report to the Department of Education on the year-to-year improvements of participating students. The independent research organization must analyze and report student performance data in a manner that protects the rights of students and parents as mandated in 20 U.S.C. s. 1232g, the Family Educational Rights and Privacy Act, and must not disaggregate data to a level that will disclose the academic level of individual students or of individual schools. To the extent possible, the independent research organization must accumulate historical performance data on students from the Department of Education and private schools to describe baseline performance and to conduct longitudinal studies. To minimize costs and reduce time required for third-party analysis and evaluation, the Department of Education shall conduct analyses of matched students from public school assessment data and calculate control group learning gains using an agreed-upon methodology outlined in the contract with the third-party evaluator. The sharing of student data must be in accordance with requirements of 20 U.S.C. s. 1232g, the Family Educational Rights and Privacy Act, and shall be for the sole purpose of conducting the evaluation. All parties must preserve the confidentiality of such information as required by law.

(k) Notify an eligible nonprofit scholarship-funding organization of any of the organization's identified students who are receiving educational scholarships pursuant to chapter 1002.

(l) Notify an eligible nonprofit scholarship-funding organization of any of the organization's identified students who are receiving corporate income tax credit scholarships from other eligible nonprofit scholarship-funding organizations.

(m) Require quarterly reports by an eligible nonprofit scholarship-funding organization regarding the number of students participating in the scholarship program, the private schools at which the students are enrolled, and other information deemed necessary by the Department of Education.

(n)
   1. Conduct random site visits to private schools participating in the Corporate Tax Credit Scholarship Program. The purpose of the site visits is solely to verify the information reported by the schools concerning the enrollment and attendance of students, the credentials of teachers, background screening of teachers,

and teachers' fingerprinting results. The Department of Education may not make more than seven random site visits each year and may not make more than one random site visit each year to the same private school.

2. Annually, by December 15, report to the Governor, the President of the Senate, and the Speaker of the House of Representatives the Department of Education's actions with respect to implementing accountability in the scholarship program under this section and s. 1002.421, any substantiated allegations or violations of law or rule by an eligible private school under this program concerning the enrollment and attendance of students, the credentials of teachers, background screening of teachers, and teachers' fingerprinting results and the corrective action taken by the Department of Education.

(10) COMMISSIONER OF EDUCATION AUTHORITY AND OBLIGATIONS.—

(a) The Commissioner of Education shall deny, suspend, or revoke a private school's participation in the scholarship program if it is determined that the private school has failed to comply with the provisions of this section. However, in instances in which the noncompliance is correctable within a reasonable amount of time and in which the health, safety, or welfare of the students is not threatened, the commissioner may issue a notice of noncompliance that shall provide the private school with a timeframe within which to provide evidence of compliance prior to taking action to suspend or revoke the private school's participation in the scholarship program.

(b) The commissioner's determination is subject to the following:

1. If the commissioner intends to deny, suspend, or revoke a private school's participation in the scholarship program, the Department of Education shall notify the private school of such proposed action in writing by certified mail and regular mail to the private school's address of record with the Department of Education. The notification shall include the reasons for the proposed action and notice of the timelines and procedures set forth in this paragraph.

2. The private school that is adversely affected by the proposed action shall have 15 days from receipt of the notice of proposed action to file with the Department of Education's agency clerk a request for a proceeding pursuant to ss. 120.569 and 120.57. If the private school is entitled to a hearing under s. 120.57(1),

the Department of Education shall forward the request to the Division of Administrative Hearings.

3. Upon receipt of a request referred pursuant to this paragraph, the director of the Division of Administrative Hearings shall expedite the hearing and assign an administrative law judge who shall commence a hearing within 30 days after the receipt of the formal written request by the division and enter a recommended order within 30 days after the hearing or within 30 days after receipt of the hearing transcript, whichever is later. Each party shall be allowed 10 days in which to submit written exceptions to the recommended order. A final order shall be entered by the agency within 30 days after the entry of a recommended order. The provisions of this subparagraph may be waived upon stipulation by all parties.

(c) The commissioner may immediately suspend payment of scholarship funds if it is determined that there is probable cause to believe that there is:

1. An imminent threat to the health, safety, and welfare of the students; or

2. Fraudulent activity on the part of the private school. Notwithstanding s. 1002.22(3), in incidents of alleged fraudulent activity pursuant to this section, the Department of Education's Office of Inspector General is authorized to release personally identifiable records or reports of students to the following persons or organizations:

   a. A court of competent jurisdiction in compliance with an order of that court or the attorney of record in accordance with a lawfully issued subpoena, consistent with the Family Educational Rights and Privacy Act, 20 U.S.C. s. 1232g.

   b. A person or entity authorized by a court of competent jurisdiction in compliance with an order of that court or the attorney of record pursuant to a lawfully issued subpoena, consistent with the Family Educational Rights and Privacy Act, 20 U.S.C. s. 1232g.

   c. Any person, entity, or authority issuing a subpoena for law enforcement purposes when the court or other issuing agency has ordered that the existence or the contents of the subpoena or the information furnished in response to the subpoena not be disclosed, consistent with the Family Educational Rights and Privacy Act, 20 U.S.C. s. 1232g, and 34 C.F.R. s. 99.31.

The commissioner's order suspending payment pursuant to this paragraph may be appealed pursuant to the same procedures and timelines as the notice of proposed action set forth in paragraph (b).

(11) SCHOLARSHIP AMOUNT AND PAYMENT.—

(a) The amount of a scholarship provided to any student for any single school year by an eligible nonprofit scholarship-funding organization from eligible contributions shall be for total costs authorized under paragraph (6)(d), not to exceed the following annual limits:

1. Three thousand nine hundred fifty dollars for a scholarship awarded to a student enrolled in an eligible private school for the 2008–2009 state fiscal year and each fiscal year thereafter.

2. Five hundred dollars for a scholarship awarded to a student enrolled in a Florida public school that is located outside the district in which the student resides or in a lab school as defined in s. 1002.32.

(b) Payment of the scholarship by the eligible nonprofit scholarship-funding organization shall be by individual warrant made payable to the student's parent. If the parent chooses that his or her child attend an eligible private school, the warrant must be delivered by the eligible nonprofit scholarship-funding organization to the private school of the parent's choice, and the parent shall restrictively endorse the warrant to the private school. An eligible nonprofit scholarship-funding organization shall ensure that the parent to whom the warrant is made restrictively endorsed the warrant to the private school for deposit into the account of the private school.

(c) An eligible nonprofit scholarship-funding organization shall obtain verification from the private school of a student's continued attendance at the school for each period covered by a scholarship payment.

(d) Payment of the scholarship shall be made by the eligible nonprofit scholarship-funding organization no less frequently than on a quarterly basis.

(12) ADMINISTRATION; RULES.—

(a) If the credit granted pursuant to this section is not fully used in any one year because of insufficient tax liability on the part of the corporation, the unused amount may be carried forward for a period not to exceed 3 years; however, any taxpayer that seeks to carry forward an unused amount of tax credit must submit an application for allocation of tax credits or carryforward credits as required in paragraph (d) in the year that the taxpayer intends to use the carryforward. This carryforward applies to all approved contributions made after January 1, 2002. A taxpayer may not convey, assign, or transfer the credit authorized by this section to another entity unless all of the assets of the taxpayer are conveyed, assigned, or transferred in the same transaction.

(b) An application for a tax credit pursuant to this section shall be submitted to the department on forms established by rule of the department.

(c) The department and the Department of Education shall develop a cooperative agreement to assist in the administration of this section.

(d) The department shall adopt rules necessary to administer this section, including rules establishing application forms and procedures and governing the allocation of tax credits and carryforward credits under this section on a first-come, first-served basis.

(e) The State Board of Education shall adopt rules pursuant to ss. 120.536(1) and 120.54 to administer this section as it relates to the roles of the Department of Education and the Commissioner of Education.

(13) DEPOSITS OF ELIGIBLE CONTRIBUTIONS.—All eligible contributions received by an eligible nonprofit scholarship-funding organization shall be deposited in a manner consistent with s. 17.57(2).

(14) PRESERVATION OF CREDIT.—If any provision or portion of subsection (5) or the application thereof to any person or circumstance is held unconstitutional by any court or is otherwise declared invalid, the unconstitutionality or invalidity shall not affect any credit earned under subsection (5) by any taxpayer with respect to any contribution paid to an eligible nonprofit scholarship-funding organization before the date of a determination of unconstitutionality or invalidity. Such credit shall be allowed at such time and in such a manner as if a determination of unconstitutionality or invalidity had not been made, provided that nothing in this subsection by itself or in combination with any other provision of law shall result in the allowance of any credit to any taxpayer in excess of one dollar of credit for each dollar paid to an eligible nonprofit scholarship-funding organization.

Section 2. Corporate Income Tax Credit Scholarship Program funding.—

(1) By December 1, 2008, the Office of Program Policy Analysis and Government Accountability shall submit a report to the Governor, the President of the Senate, and the Speaker of the House of Representatives which:

(a) Reviews the advisability and net state fiscal impact of:

1. Increasing the maximum annual amount of credits for the corporate income tax permitted under s. 220.187, Florida Statutes, for the scholarship program.

    2. Authorizing the use of credits for insurance premium taxes under chapter 624, Florida Statutes, as an additional source of funding for the scholarship program under s. 220.187, Florida Statutes.

 (b) Provides recommendations, if warranted by the review under paragraph (a):

    1. For methodologies to annually or otherwise increase the maximum annual amount of corporate income tax credits for scholarship funding.

    2. To implement the use of insurance premium tax credits for scholarship funding.

 (c) Identifies strategies to encourage private schools that accept scholarship students to participate in the statewide assessment program under s. 1008.22, Florida Statutes. Such recommendations may only include options that will annually produce a neutral or positive net fiscal impact on state revenue and expenditures.

(2) The Office of Program Policy Analysis and Government Accountability may request that the Revenue Estimating Conference and the Education Estimating Conference established under s. 216.134, Florida Statutes, evaluate its findings and recommendations under this section.

Appendix C

Pennsylvania

Title 24, Pennsylvania Statutes (P.S.)
Educational Improvement Tax Credit

§ 20-2001-B. Scope. This article deals with the educational improvement tax credit.

§ 20-2002-B. Definitions. The following words and phrases when used in this article shall have the meanings given to them in this section unless the context clearly indicates otherwise:

"Business firm." An entity authorized to do business in this Commonwealth and subject to taxes imposed under Article IV, VI, VII, VII-A, VIII, VIII-A, IX or XV of the act of March 4, 1971 (P.L. 6, No. 2), known as the Tax Reform Code of 1971.

"Contribution." A donation of cash, personal property or services the value of which is the net cost of the donation to the donor or the pro rata hourly wage, including benefits, of the individual performing the services.

"Department." The Department of Community and Economic Development of the Commonwealth.

"Educational improvement organization." A nonprofit entity which:

(1) is exempt from Federal taxation under section 501(c)(3) of the Internal Revenue Code of 1986 (Public Law 99-514, 26 U.S.C. § 1 et seq.); and

(2) contributes at least 80% of its annual receipts as grants to a public school for innovative educational programs.

For purposes of this definition, a nonprofit entity "contributes" its annual cash receipts when it expends or otherwise irrevocably encumbers those funds for expenditure during the then current fiscal year of the nonprofit entity or during the next succeeding fiscal year of the nonprofit entity.

"Eligible pre-kindergarten student." A student who is enrolled in a pre-kindergarten program and is a member of a household with an annual household income of not more than $50,000. An income allowance of $10,000 shall be allowed for each eligible student and dependent member of the household.

"Eligible student." A school-age student who is enrolled in a school and is a member of a household with an annual household income of not more than $50,000. An income allowance of $10,000 shall be allowed for each eligible student and dependent member of the household.

"Household." An individual living alone or with the following: a spouse, parent and their unemancipated minor children; and other unemancipated minor children who are related by blood or marriage; or other adults or unemancipated minor children living in the household who are dependent upon the individual.

"Household income." All moneys or property received of whatever nature and from whatever source derived. The term does not include the following:

(1) Periodic payments for sickness and disability other than regular wages received during a period of sickness or disability.

(2) Disability, retirement or other payments arising under workers' compensation acts, occupational disease acts and similar legislation by any government.

(3) Payments commonly recognized as old-age or retirement benefits paid to persons retired from service after reaching a specific age or after a stated period of employment.

(4) Payments commonly known as public assistance or unemployment compensation payments by a governmental agency.

(5) Payments to reimburse actual expenses.

(6) Payments made by employers or labor unions for programs covering hospitalization, sickness, disability or death, supplemental unemployment benefits, strike benefits, Social Security and retirement.

(7) Compensation received by United States servicemen serving in a combat zone.

"Innovative educational program." An advanced academic or similar program that is not part of the regular academic program of a public school but that enhances the curriculum or academic program of the public school.

"Pre-kindergarten program." A program of instruction for three-year-old or four-year-old students that utilizes a curriculum aligned with the curriculum of the school with which it is affiliated and which provides a minimum of two hours of instructional and developmental activities per day at least 60 days per school year.

"Pre-kindergarten scholarship organization." A nonprofit entity which:

(1) either is exempt from Federal taxation under section 501(c)(3) of the Internal Revenue Code of 1986 (Public Law 99-514, 26 U.S.C. § 1 et seq.) or is operated as a separate segregated fund by a scholarship organization that has been qualified under section 2003-B; and

(2) contributes at least 80% of its annual cash receipts to a pre-kindergarten scholarship program by expending or otherwise irrevocably encumbering those funds for distribution during the then current fiscal year of the organization or during the next succeeding fiscal year of the organization.

"Pre-kindergarten scholarship program." A program to provide tuition to eligible pre-kindergarten students to attend a pre-kindergarten program operated by or in conjunction with a school located in this Commonwealth and that includes an application and review process for the purpose of making awards to eligible pre-kindergarten students and awards scholarships to eligible pre-kindergarten students without limiting availability to only students of one school.

"Public school." A public kindergarten, elementary school or secondary school at which the compulsory attendance requirements of this Commonwealth may be met and which meets the applicable requirements of Title VI of the Civil Rights Act of 1964 (Public Law 88-352, 78 Stat. 241).

"Scholarship organization." A nonprofit entity which:

(1) is exempt from Federal taxation under section 501(c)(3) of the Internal Revenue Code of 1986 (Public Law 99-514, 26 U.S.C. § 1 et seq.); and

(2) contributes at least 80% of its annual cash receipts to a scholarship program.

For purposes of this definition, a nonprofit entity "contributes" its annual cash receipts to a scholarship program when it expends or otherwise irrevocably encumbers those funds for distribution during the then current fiscal year of the nonprofit entity or during the next succeeding fiscal year of the nonprofit entity.

"Scholarship program." A program to provide tuition to eligible students to attend a school located in this Commonwealth. A scholarship program must include an application and review process for the purpose of making awards to eligible students. The award of scholarships to eligible students shall be made without limiting availability to only students of one school.

"School." A public or nonpublic kindergarten, elementary school or secondary school at which the compulsory attendance requirements of the Commonwealth may be met and which meets the applicable requirements of Title VI of the Civil Rights Act of 1964 (Public Law 88-352, 78 Stat. 241).

"School age." Children from the earliest admission age to a school's pre-kindergarten or kindergarten program or, when no pre-kindergarten or kindergarten program is provided, the school's earliest admission age for beginners, until the end of the school year the student attains 21 years of age or graduation from high school, whichever occurs first.

§ 20-2003-B. Qualification and application

(a) ESTABLISHMENT.—In accordance with section 14 of Article III of the Constitution of Pennsylvania, an **educational improvement tax credit** program is hereby established to enhance the educational opportunities available to all students in this Commonwealth.

(b) INFORMATION.—In order to qualify under this article, a scholarship organization, a pre-kindergarten scholarship organization or an educational improvement organization must submit information to the department that enables the department to confirm that the organization is exempt from taxation under section 501(c)(3) of the Internal Revenue Code of 1986 (Public Law 99-514, 26 U.S.C. § 1 et seq.).

(c) SCHOLARSHIP ORGANIZATIONS AND PRE-KINDERGARTEN SCHOLARSHIP ORGANIZATIONS.—A scholarship organization or pre-kindergarten scholarship organization must certify to the department that the organization is eligible to participate in the program established under this article and must agree to annually report the following information to the department by December 1, 2005, and September 1 of each year thereafter:

(1)

    (i)   The number of scholarships awarded during the immediately preceding school year to eligible pre-kindergarten students.

    (ii)   The total and average amounts of the scholarships awarded during the immediately preceding school year to eligible pre-kindergarten students.

(iii) The number of scholarships awarded during the immediately preceding school year to eligible students in grades K through 8.

(iv) The total and average amounts of the scholarships awarded during the immediately preceding school year to eligible students in grades K through 8.

(v) The number of scholarships awarded during the immediately preceding school year to eligible students in grades 9 through 12.

(vi) The total and average amounts of the scholarships awarded during the immediately preceding school year to eligible students in grades 9 through 12.

(vii) Where the scholarship organization or pre-kindergarten scholarship organization collects information on a county-by-county basis, the total number and the total amount of scholarships awarded during the immediately preceding school year to residents of each county in which the scholarship organization or pre-kindergarten scholarship organization awarded scholarships.

(2) The information required under paragraph (1) shall be submitted on a form provided by the department. No later than September 1, 2005, and May 1 of each year thereafter, the department shall annually distribute such sample forms, together with the forms on which the reports are required to be made, to each listed scholarship organization and pre-kindergarten scholarship organization.

(3) The department may not require any other information to be provided by scholarship organizations or pre-kindergarten scholarship organizations, except as expressly authorized in this article.

(d) EDUCATIONAL IMPROVEMENT ORGANIZATION.—

(1) An application submitted by an educational improvement organization must describe its proposed innovative educational program or programs in a form prescribed by the department. The department shall consult with the Department of Education as necessary. The department shall review and approve or disapprove the application. In order to be eligible to participate in the program established under this article, an educational improvement organization must agree to annually report the following information to the department by December 1, 2005, and September 1 of each year thereafter:

(i) The name of the innovative educational program or programs and the total amount of the grant or grants made to those programs during the immediately preceding school year.

(ii)   A description of how each grant was utilized during the immediately preceding school year and a description of any demonstrated or expected innovative educational improvements.

(iii) The names of the public schools and school districts where innovative educational programs that received grants during the immediately preceding school year were implemented.

(iv)   Where the educational improvement organization collects information on a county-by-county basis, the total number and the total amount of grants made during the immediately preceding school year for programs at public schools in each county in which the educational improvement organization made grants.

(2) The information required under paragraph (1) shall be submitted on a form provided by the department. No later than September 1, 2005, and May 1 of each year thereafter, the department shall annually distribute such sample forms, together with the forms on which the reports are required to be made, to each listed educational improvement organization.

(3) The department may not require any other information to be provided by educational improvement organizations, except as expressly authorized in this article.

(e) NOTIFICATION.—The department shall notify the scholarship organization, pre-kindergarten scholarship organization or educational improvement organization that the organization meets the requirements of this article for that fiscal year no later than 60 days after the organization has submitted the information required under this section.

(f) PUBLICATION.—The department shall annually publish a list of each scholarship organization, pre-kindergarten scholarship organization or educational improvement organization qualified under this section in the Pennsylvania Bulletin. The list shall also be posted and updated as necessary on the publicly accessible World Wide Web site of the department.

§ 20-2004-B. Application

(a) SCHOLARSHIP ORGANIZATION OR PRE-KINDERGARTEN SCHOLARSHIP ORGANIZATIONS.—A business firm shall apply to the department for a tax credit under section 2005-B. A business firm shall receive a tax credit under this article if the scholarship organization or pre-kindergarten scholarship organization that receives the contribution appears on the list established under section 2003-B(f).

(b) EDUCATIONAL IMPROVEMENT ORGANIZATION.—A business firm must apply to the department for a credit under section 2005-B. A business firm shall receive a tax credit under this article if the department has approved the program provided by the educational improvement organization that receives the contribution.

(c) AVAILABILITY OF TAX CREDITS.—Tax credits under this article shall be made available by the department on a first-come, first-served basis within the limitation established under section 2006-B(a).

(d) CONTRIBUTIONS.—A contribution by a business firm to a scholarship organization, pre-kindergarten scholarship organization or educational improvement organization shall be made no later than 60 days following the approval of an application under subsection (a) or (b).

§ 20-2005-B. Tax credit

(a) SCHOLARSHIP OR EDUCATIONAL IMPROVEMENT ORGANIZATIONS.—In accordance with section 2006-B(a), the Department of Revenue shall grant a tax credit against any tax due under Article IV, VI, VII, VII-A, VIII, VIII-A, IX or XV of the act of March 4, 1971 (P.L. 6, No. 2), known as the Tax Reform Code of 1971, to a business firm providing proof of a contribution to a scholarship organization or educational improvement organization in the taxable year in which the contribution is made which shall not exceed 75% of the total amount contributed during the taxable year by the business firm. Such credit shall not exceed $200,000 annually per business firm for contributions made to scholarship organizations or educational improvement organizations.

(b) ADDITIONAL AMOUNT.—The Department of Revenue shall grant a tax credit of up to 90% of the total amount contributed during the taxable year if the business firm provides a written commitment to provide the scholarship organization or educational improvement organization with the same amount of contribution for two consecutive tax years. The business firm must provide the written commitment under this subsection to the department at the time of application.

(c) PRE-KINDERGARTEN SCHOLARSHIP ORGANIZATIONS.—In accordance with section 2006-B(a), the Department of Revenue shall grant a tax credit against any tax due under Article IV, VI, VII, VII-A, VIII, VIII-A, IX or XV of the "Tax Reform Code of 1971" to a business firm providing proof of a contribution to a pre-kindergarten scholarship organization in the taxable year in which the contribution is made which shall be equal to 100% of the first $10,000 contributed during the taxable year by the business firm, and which shall not exceed 90% of the remaining amount contributed during the taxable year by the business firm. Such credit shall not exceed $100,000 annually per business firm for contributions made to pre-kindergarten scholarship organizations.

(d) COMBINATION OF TAX CREDITS.—A business firm may receive tax credits from the Department of Revenue in any tax year for any combination of contributions under subsection (a) or (b) or (c). In no case may a business firm receive tax credits in any tax year in excess of $200,000 for contributions under subsection (a) and (b). In no case shall a business firm receive tax credits in any tax year in excess of $100,000 for contributions under subsection (c).

§ 20-2006-B. Limitations

(a) AMOUNT.—

(1) The total aggregate amount of all tax credits approved shall not exceed $44,000,000 in a fiscal year. No less than $29,333,333 of the total aggregate amount shall be used to provide tax credits for contributions from business firms to scholarship organizations. No less than $14,666,666 of the total aggregate amount shall be used to provide tax credits for contributions from business firms to educational improvement organizations.

(2) For the fiscal year 2004–2005 and each fiscal year thereafter, the total aggregate amount of all tax credits approved for contributions from business firms to pre-kindergarten scholarship programs shall not exceed $5,000,000 in a fiscal year.

(b) ACTIVITIES.—No tax credit shall be approved for activities that are a part of a business firm's normal course of business.

(c) TAX LIABILITY.—A tax credit granted for any one taxable year may not exceed the tax liability of a business firm.

(d) USE.—A tax credit not used in the taxable year the contribution was made may not be carried forward or carried back and is not refundable or transferable.

(e) NONTAXABLE INCOME.—A scholarship received by an eligible student or eligible pre-kindergarten student shall not be considered to be taxable income for the purposes of Article III of the act of March 4, 1971 (P.L. 6, No. 2), known as the Tax Reform Code of 1971.

§ 20-2007-B. Lists

The Department of Revenue shall provide a list of all scholarship organizations, pre-kindergarten scholarship organizations and educational improvement organizations receiving contributions from business firms granted a tax credit under this article to the General Assembly by June 30 of each year.

§ 20-2008-B. Guidelines

The department in consultation with the Department of Education shall develop guidelines to determine the eligibility of an innovative educational program.

Appendix D

Iowa

Iowa § 701-42.30(422)
School Tuition Organization Tax Credit

Effective for tax years beginning on or after January 1, 2006, a school tuition organization tax credit is available which is equal to 65 percent of the amount of the voluntary cash contributions made by a taxpayer to a school tuition organization.

42.30(1) Definitions. The following definitions are applicable to this rule:
"Certified enrollment" means the enrollment at schools served by school tuition organizations as of the third Friday of September of the appropriate year.
"Contribution" means a voluntary cash contribution to a school tuition organization that is not used for the direct benefit of any dependent of the taxpayer or any other student designated by the taxpayer.
"Eligible student" means a student residing in Iowa who is a member of a household whose total annual income during the calendar year prior to the school year in which the student receives a tuition grant from a school tuition organization does not exceed an amount equal to three times the most recently published federal poverty guidelines in the Federal Register by the United States Department of Health and Human Services.
"Qualified school" means a nonpublic elementary or secondary school in Iowa which is accredited under Iowa Code section 256.11 and adheres to the provisions of the federal Civil Rights Act of 1964 and Iowa Code

chapter 216, and which is represented by only one school tuition organization.

"School tuition organization" means a charitable organization in Iowa that is exempt from federal taxation under Section 501(c)(3) of the Internal Revenue Code and that does all of the following:

1. Allocates at least 90 percent of its annual revenue in tuition grants for children to allow them to attend a qualified school of their parents' choice.
2. Awards tuition grants only to children who reside in Iowa.
3. Provides tuition grants to students without limiting availability to students of only one school.
4. Provides tuition grants only to eligible students.
5. Prepares an annual financial statement certified by a public accounting firm.

"Tuition grant" means a grant to a student to cover all or part of the student's tuition at a qualified school.

42.30(2) Initial registration. In order for contributions to a school tuition organization to qualify for the credit, the school tuition organization must initially register with the department. The following information must be provided with this initial registration:

a. Verification from the Internal Revenue Service that Section 501(c)(3) status was granted and that the school tuition organization is exempt from federal income tax.
b. A list of all qualified schools that the school tuition organization serves.
c. The names and addresses of the seven members of the board of directors of the school tuition organization.

Once the school tuition organization is registered with the department, it is not required to subsequently register unless there is a change in the qualified schools that the organization serves. The school tuition organization must notify the department by letter of any changes in the qualified schools it serves.

42.30(3) Participation forms. Each qualified school that is served by a school tuition organization must annually submit a participation form to the department by October 15. The following information must be provided with this participation form:

a. The certified enrollment of the qualified school as of the third Friday of September.
b. The name of the school tuition organization that represents the qualified school.

For the tax year beginning in the 2006 calendar year only, each qualified school served by a school tuition organization must submit to the department a participation form postmarked on or before August 1, 2006, which provides the certified enrollment as of the third Friday of September 2005, along with the name of the school tuition organization that represents the qualified school.

42.30(4) Authorization to issue tax credit certificates.

    a. By November 15 of each year, the department will authorize school tuition organizations to issue tax credit certificates for the following tax year. For the tax year beginning in the 2006 calendar year only, the department, by September 1, 2006, will authorize school tuition organizations to issue tax credit certificates for the 2006 calendar year only. The total amount of tax credit certificates that may be authorized is $2.5 million for the 2006 calendar year and $5.0 million for the 2007 and subsequent calendar years.

    b. The amount of authorized tax credit certificates for each school tuition organization is determined by dividing the total amount of tax credit available by the total certified enrollment of all qualified participating schools. This result, which is the per-student tax credit, is then multiplied by the certified enrollment of each school tuition organization to determine the tax credit authorized to each school tuition organization.

Example: For determining the authorized tax credits for the 2007 calendar year, if the certified enrollment of each qualified school in Iowa, as provided to the department by October 15, 2006, were 25,000, the per-student tax credit would be $200 ($5 million divided by 25,000). If a school tuition organization located in Scott County represents four qualified schools with a certified enrollment of 1,400 students, the school tuition organization would be authorized to issue $280,000 ($200 times 1,400) of tax credit certificates for the 2007 calendar year. The department would notify this school tuition organization by November 15, 2006, of the authorization to issue $280,000 of tax credit certificates for the 2007 calendar year. This authorization would allow the school tuition organization to solicit contributions totaling $430,769 ($280,000 divided by 65%) during the 2007 calendar year which would be eligible for the tax credit.

42.30(5) Issuance of tax credit certificates. The school tuition organization shall issue tax credit certificates to each taxpayer who made a cash contribution to the school tuition organization. The tax credit certificate, which will be designed by the department, will contain the name, address and tax identification number of the taxpayer, the amount and date that the contribution was made, the amount of the credit, the tax year that the credit may be applied, the school tuition organization to which the contribution was made, and the tax credit certificate number.

42.30(6) Claiming the tax credit. The taxpayer must attach the tax credit certificate to the tax return for which the credit is claimed. Any credit in excess of the tax liability for the tax year may be credited to the tax liability for the following five years or until used, whichever is the earlier.

a. The taxpayer may not claim an itemized deduction for charitable contributions for Iowa income tax purposes for the amount of the contribution made to the school tuition organization.

b. Married taxpayers who file separate returns or file separately on a combined return must allocate the school tuition organization tax credit to each spouse in the proportion that each spouse's respective net income bears to the total combined net income. Nonresidents or part-year residents of Iowa must determine the school tuition organization tax credit in the ratio of their Iowa source net income to their total source net income. In addition, if nonresidents or part-year residents of Iowa are married and elect to file separate returns or to file separately on a combined return, the school tuition organization tax credit must be allocated between the spouses in the ratio of each spouse's Iowa source net income to the combined Iowa source net income.

42.30(7) Reporting requirements. Each school tuition organization that issues tax credit certificates must report to the department, postmarked by January 12 of each tax year, the following information:

a. The names and addresses of the seven members of the board of directors of the school tuition organization, along with the name of the chairperson of the board.

b. The total number and dollar value of contributions received by the school tuition organization for the previous tax year.

c. The total number and dollar value of tax credit certificates issued by the school tuition organization for the previous tax year.

d. A list of each taxpayer who received a tax credit certificate for the previous tax year, including the amount of the contribution and the amount of tax credit issued to each taxpayer for the previous tax year. This list should also include the tax identification number of the taxpayer and the tax credit certificate number for each certificate.

e. The total number of children utilizing tuition grants for the school year in progress as of January 12, along with the total dollar value of the tuition grants.

f. The name and address of each qualified school represented by the school tuition organization at which tuition grants are being utilized for the school year in progress.

g. The number of tuition grant students and the total dollar value of tuition grants being utilized for the school year in progress at each qualified school served by the school tuition organization.

Appendix E

Rhode Island

Chapter 44-62
Tax Credits for Contributions to Scholarship Organizations

§ 44-62-1 Tax credit for contributions to a scholarship organization—General. [Effective January 1, 2007.].—In order to enhance the educational opportunities available to all students in this state, a business entity will be allowed a tax credit to be computed as provided in this chapter for voluntary cash contribution made by the business entity to a qualified scholarship.

§ 44-62-2 Qualification of scholarship organization. [Effective January 1, 2007.].—A scholarship organization must certify annually by December 31st to the division of taxation that the organization is eligible to participate in the program in accordance with criteria as defined below:

(a) "Scholarship organization" means a charitable organization in this state that is exempt from federal taxation under § 501(c)(3) of the internal revenue code, and that allocates at least ninety percent (90%) of its annual revenue through a scholarship program for tuition assistance grants to eligible students to allow them to attend any qualified school of their parents' choice represented by the scholarship organization.

(b) "Scholarship program" means a program to provide tuition assistance grants to eligible students to attend a nonpublic school located in this state. A scholarship program must include an application and review process for the purpose of making these grants only to eligible students. The award of scholarships to eligible students shall be made without limiting availability to only students of one school.

(c) "Eligible student" means a school-age student who is registered in a qualified school and is a member of a household with an annual household income of not more than two hundred fifty percent (250%) of the federal poverty guidelines as published in the federal register by the United States Department of Health and Human Services.

(d) "Household" means one or more persons occupying a dwelling unit and living as a single nonprofit housekeeping unit. Household does not mean bona fide lessees, tenants, or roomers and borders on contract.

(e) "Household income" means all income received by all persons of a household in a calendar year while members of the household.

(f) "Income" means the sum of federal adjusted gross income as defined in the internal revenue code of the United States, 26 U.S.C. § 1 et seq., and all nontaxable income including, but not limited to, the amount of capital gains excluded from adjusted gross income, alimony, support money, nontaxable strike benefits, cash public assistance and relief (not including relief granted under this chapter), the gross amount of any pension or annuity (including Railroad Retirement Act (see 45 U.S.C. § 231 et seq.) benefits), all payments received under the federal Social Security Act, 42 U.S.C. § 301 et seq., state unemployment insurance laws, and veterans' disability pensions (see 38 U.S.C. § 301 et seq.), nontaxable interest received from the federal government or any of its instrumentalities, workers' compensation, and the gross amount of "loss of time" insurance. It does not include gifts from nongovernmental sources, or surplus foods or other relief in kind supplied by a public or private agency.

(g) "Qualified school" means a nonpublic elementary or secondary school that is located in this state and that satisfies the requirements prescribed by law for nonpublic schools in this state.

(h) "School-age student" means a child at the earliest admission age to a qualified school's kindergarten program or, when no kindergarten program is provided, the school's earliest admission age for beginners, until the end of the school year, the student attains twenty-one (21) years of age or graduation from high school whichever occurs first.

(i) Designation. A donation to a scholarship organization, for which the donor receives a tax credit under this provision, may not be designated to any specific school or student by the donor.

(j) Nontaxable income. A scholarship received by an eligible student shall not be considered to be taxable income.

§ 44-62-3 Application for the tax credit program. [Effective January 1, 2007.].—

(a) Prior to the contribution, a business entity shall apply in writing to the division of taxation. The application shall contain such information and certification as the tax administrator deems necessary for the proper administration of this chapter. A business entity shall be approved if it meets the criteria of this chapter; the dollar amount of the applied for tax credit is no greater than one hundred thousand dollars ($100,000) in any tax year, and the scholarship organization which is to receive the contribution has qualified under § 44-62-2.

(b) Approvals for contributions under this section shall be made available by the division of taxation on a first-come-first-serve basis. The total aggregate amount of all tax credits approved shall not exceed one million dollars ($1,000,000) in a fiscal year.

(c) The division of taxation shall notify the business entity in writing within thirty (30) days of the receipt of application of the division's approval or rejection of the application.

(d) Unless the contribution is part of a two-year plan, the actual cash contribution by the business entity to a qualified scholarship organization must be made no later than one hundred twenty (120) days following the approval of its application. If the contribution is part of a two-year plan, the first year's contribution follows the general rule and the second year's contribution must be made in the subsequent calendar year by the same date.

(e) The contributions must be those charitable contributions made in cash as set forth in the Internal Revenue Code.

§ 44-62-4 Calculation of tax credit and issuance of tax credit certificate. [Effective January 1, 2007.].—

(a) When the contribution has been made as set forth in section 3 above, the business entity shall apply to the division of taxation for a tax credit certificate. The application will include such information, documentation, and certification as the tax administrator deems proper for the administration of this chapter including, but not limited to a certification by an independent Rhode Island certified public accountant that the cash contribution has actually been made to the qualified scholarship organization. For purposes of the proper administration of this section, an independent Rhode Island certified public accountant shall be licensed in accordance with RIGL 5-3.1 and means a person, partnership, corporation, limited liability corporation that is not affiliated with or an employee of said business entity or its affiliates and is not affiliated in any manner whatsoever with a qualified scholarship organization or scholarship program as defined in § 42-62-2 (a)—(j).

(b) The division of taxation will review the documentation submitted; calculate the tax credit pertaining to the contribution, and prepare and mail a certificate for amount of credit to be granted.

(c) Unless a two year contribution plan is in place, the credit is computed at seventy-five percent (75%) of the total voluntary cash contribution made by the business entity.

(d) The credit is available against taxes otherwise due under provisions of chapters 11, 13, 14, 15 or 17 of this title.

(e)

(1) A two year contribution plan is based on the written commitment of the business entity to provide the scholarship organization with the same amount of contribution for two (2) consecutive tax years. The business entity must provide in writing a commitment to this extended contribution to the scholarship organization and the division of taxation at the time of application.

(2) In the event that a two year contribution plan is in place, the calculation of credit for each year shall be ninety percent (90%) of the total voluntary contribution made by a business entity.

(3) In the event that, in the second year of the plan, a business entity's contribution falls below the contribution amount made in the first year but the second year's contribution is eighty percent (80%) or greater than the first year's contribution, the business entity shall receive a credit for both the first and second year contributions equal to ninety percent (90%) of each year's contribution.

(4) If the amount of the second year contribution is less than eighty percent (80%) of the first year contribution, then the credit for both the first and second year contributions shall be equal to seventy-five percent (75%) of each year's contribution. In such case, the tax administrator shall prepare the tax credit certificate for the second year at seventy-five percent (75%). The difference in credit allowable for the first year [90% − 75% = 15% x first year contribution] shall be recaptured by adding it to the taxpayer's tax in that year.

§ 44-62-5 Limitations. [Effective January 1, 2007.].—

(a) The credit shall not exceed one hundred thousand dollars ($100,000) annually per business entity.

(b) The tax credit must be used in the tax year the contribution was made. Any amounts of unused tax credit may not be carried forward. The tax credit is not refundable, assignable or transferable. The tax credit may not reduce the tax below the state minimum tax.

(c) The credit allowed under this chapter is only allowed against the tax of that corporation included in a consolidated return that qualifies for the credit and not against the tax of other corporations that may join in the filing of a consolidated tax return.

§ 44-62-6 Definitions. [Effective January 1, 2007.].—The following words and phrases used in this chapter shall have the meanings given to them in this section unless the context clearly indicates otherwise:

(1) "Business entity" means an entity authorized to do business in this state and subject to taxes imposed under chapters 44-11, 44-13, 44-14, 44-15 and 44-17 of the general laws.

(2) "Division of taxation" means the Rhode Island division of taxation.

§ 44-62-7 Miscellaneous—Lists. [Effective January 1, 2007.].—By June 30 of each year, the division of taxation shall annually publish in print and on the division of taxation's website a list of all qualified scholarship organizations under § 44-62-4. The list will indicate which scholarship organizations received contributions from business entities for which tax credits were authorized under this chapter. In addition, each scholarship organization shall submit to the division of taxation by December 31st of each year the following information, which shall be a public record: the number of scholarships distributed by the organization, per school, and the dollar range of those scholarships; a breakdown by zip code of the place of residence for each student receiving a scholarship under this program; and a description of all criteria used by the organization in determining to whom scholarships under this program shall be awarded.

Appendix F

Georgia House Bill 1133 (2008)

[Note: Because the law was enacted just as this book was going to press, the Bill (rather than the statute) is presented here.]

BE IT ENACTED BY THE GENERAL ASSEMBLY OF GEORGIA:

SECTION 1.
Title 20 of the Official Code of Georgia Annotated, relating to education, is amended by adding a new chapter to read as follows:

CHAPTER 2A
20-2A-1.
As used in this chapter, the term:
  (1) 'Eligible student' means a student who is a Georgia resident enrolled in a Georgia secondary or primary public school or eligible to enroll in a qualified kindergarten program or pre-kindergarten program.
  (2) 'Qualified school or program' means a nonpublic primary school or secondary school that:
    (A) Is accredited or in the process of becoming accredited by one or more entities listed in subparagraph (A) of paragraph (6) of Code Section 20-3-519; and
    (B) Is located in this state, adheres to the provisions of the federal Civil Rights Act of 1964, and satisfies the requirements prescribed by law for private schools in this state.

(3) 'Student scholarship organization' means a charitable organization in this state that:
  (A) Is exempt from federal income taxation under Section 501(c)(3) of the Internal Revenue Code and allocates 90 percent of its annual revenue for scholarships or tuition grants to allow students to attend any qualified school of their parents' choice; and
  (B) Provides educational scholarships or tuition grants to eligible students without limiting availability to only students of one school.

20-2A-2.

Each student scholarship organization:
  (1) Must obligate 90 percent of its annual revenue for scholarships or tuition grants; however, up to 25 percent of this amount may be carried forward for the next fiscal year;
  (2) Must maintain separate accounts for scholarship funds and operating funds;
  (3) May transfer funds to another student scholarship organization;
  (4) Must conduct an audit of its accounts by an independent certified public accountant within 120 days after the completion of the student scholarship organization's fiscal year and provide such audit to the Department of Revenue in accordance with Code Section 20-2A-3; and
  (5) Must annually submit notice to the Department of Education in accordance with department guidelines of its participation as a student scholarship organization under this chapter.

20-2A-3.

  (a) Each student scholarship organization must report to the Department of Revenue, on a form provided by the Department of Revenue, by January 12 of each tax year the following:
    (1) The total number and dollar value of contributions and tax credits approved; and
    (2) A list of donors, including the dollar value of each donation and the dollar value of each approved tax credit.
    Such report shall also include a copy of the audit conducted pursuant to paragraph (4) of Code Section 20-2A-2.
  (b) The Department of Revenue shall not require any other information from student scholarship organizations, except as expressly authorized in this chapter.

20-2A-4.

The Department of Revenue shall provide a list of all student scholarship organizations receiving contributions from businesses and individuals granted a tax credit under Code Section 48-7-29.13 to the General Assembly by January 30 of each year.

20-2A-5.
The parent or guardian to whom a scholarship award is granted must restrictively endorse the scholarship award to the private school for deposit into the account of the private school. The parent or guardian may not designate any entity or individual associated with the participating private school as the parent's attorney in fact to endorse a scholarship warrant. A participant who fails to comply with this Code section forfeits the scholarship.

20-2A-6.
The Department of Education shall maintain on its website a current list of all student scholarship organizations which have provided notice pursuant to paragraph (5) of Code Section 20-2A-2.

SECTION 2.
Title 48 of the Official Code of Georgia Annotated, relating to revenue and taxation, is amended by adding a new Code section to read as follows:

48-7-29.13.
   (a) As used in this Code section, the term:
       (1) 'Qualified education expense' means the expenditure of funds by the taxpayer during the tax year for which a credit under this Code section is claimed and allowed to a student scholarship organization operating pursuant to Chapter 2A of Title 20 which are used for tuition and fees for a qualified school or program.
       (2) 'Qualified school or program' shall have the same meaning as in paragraph (2) of Code Section 20-2A-1.
       (3) 'Student scholarship organization' shall have the same meaning as in paragraph (3) of Code Section 20-2A-1.
   (b) An individual taxpayer shall be allowed a credit against the tax imposed by this chapter for qualified education expenses as follows:
       (1) In the case of a single individual or a head of household, the actual amount expended or $1,000.00 per tax year, whichever is less; or
       (2) In the case of a married couple filing a joint return, the actual amount expended or $2,500.00 per tax year, whichever is less.
   (c) A corporation shall be allowed a credit against the tax imposed by this chapter for qualified education expenses in an amount not to exceed the actual amount expended or 75 percent of the corporation's income tax liability, whichever is less.

(d) The tax credit shall not be allowed if the taxpayer designates the taxpayer's qualified education expense for the direct benefit of any dependent of the taxpayer.

(e) In no event shall the total amount of the tax credit under this Code section for a taxable year exceed the taxpayer's income tax liability. Any unused tax credit shall be allowed the taxpayer against the succeeding five years' tax liability. No such credit shall be allowed the taxpayer against prior years' tax liability.

(f) (1) In no event shall the aggregate amount of tax credits allowed under this Code section exceed $50 million per tax year.

  (2) The commissioner shall allow the tax credits on a first come, first served basis.

  (3) For the purposes of paragraph (1) of this subsection, a student scholarship organization shall notify a potential donor of the requirements of this Code section. Before making a contribution to a student scholarship organization, the taxpayer shall notify the department of the total amount of contributions that the taxpayer intends to make to the student scholarship organization. The commissioner shall preapprove or deny the requested amount within 30 days after receiving the request from the taxpayer. In order to receive a tax credit under this Code section, the taxpayer shall make the contribution to the student scholarship organization within 30 days after receiving notice from the department that the requested amount was preapproved. If the taxpayer does not comply with this paragraph, the commissioner shall not include this preapproved contribution amount when calculating the limit prescribed in paragraph (1) of this subsection.

  (4) Preapproval of contributions by the commissioner shall be based solely on the availability of tax credits subject to the aggregate total limit established under paragraph (1) of this subsection.

(g) In order for the taxpayer to claim the student scholarship organization tax credit under this Code section, a letter of confirmation of donation issued by the student scholarship organization to which the contribution was made shall be attached to the taxpayer's tax return. The letter of confirmation of donation shall contain the taxpayer's name, address, tax identification number, the amount of the contribution, the date of the contribution, and the amount of the credit.

(h) (1) No credit shall be allowed under this Code section with respect to any amount deducted from taxable net income by the taxpayer as a charitable contribution to a bona fide charitable organization qualified under Section 501(c)(3) of the Internal Revenue Code.

(2) The amount of any scholarship received by an eligible student or eligible pre-kindergarten student shall be excluded from taxable net income for Georgia income tax purposes.

(i) The commissioner shall be authorized to promulgate any rules and regulations necessary to implement and administer the tax provisions of this Code section.

SECTION 3.

This Act shall become effective upon its approval by the Governor or upon its becoming law without such approval and shall be applicable to all taxable years beginning on or after January 1, 2008.

SECTION 4.

All laws and parts of laws in conflict with this Act are repealed.

References

Abington Township School District v. Schempp, 374 U.S. 203 (1963).

Acevedo-Delgado v. Rivera, 292 F.3d. 37 (1ˢᵗ Cir. 2002).

Agostini v. Felton, 521 U.S. 203 (1997).

Aguilar v. Felton, 473 U.S. 402 (1985).

Allgood, W., and Rice, J. K. (2002). The adequacy of urban education: Focusing on teacher quality. In *Fiscal Policy in Urban Education*, ed. Christopher Roellke and Jennifer Rice King, 155–180. Greenwich, CT: Information Age Publishing.

Alliance for School Choice (2007a). *School choice around the nation: Florida's Step Up for Students Scholarship Program.* Retrieved November 24, 2007, from www.allianceforschoolchoice.org/more.aspx?IICatID=0&IIID=2911.

———. (2007b). *School Choice around the nation: Pennsylvania's Education Improvement Tax Credit Program.* Retrieved November 24, 2007, from www.allianceforschoolchoice.org/more.aspx?IICatID=0&IIID=2906.

Anderson v. Town of Durham, No. CV-02-480 (Cumberland County Superior Court, Maine) (2002).

Andrews, L. M. (2002, July 7). Cleveland's impact on Connecticut schools. *The Hartford Courant*, p. C1.

Arizona Department of Revenue (2006). *Individual income tax credit for donations to private school tuition organizations: Reporting for 2005.* Retrieved June 17, 2006, from www.azdor.gov/OERA/private_schl_credit_report_2006.pdf.

———. (2007). *Arizona income tax credits.* Retrieved November 23, 2007, from www.azdor.gov/Refunds%20and%20Credits/credithistoryofficialrelease07.pdf.

———. (2008). *Individual income tax credit for donations to private school tuition organizations: Reporting for 2007.* Retrieved July 7, 2008, from www.revenue.state.az.us/ResearchStats/private_schl_credit_report_2007.pdf.

Arsen, D., Plank, D., and Sykes, G. (2000). *School choice policies in Michigan: The rules matter.* East Lansing: Michigan State University.

Asociación de Maestros v. Torres, 137 D.P.R. 528, 1994 PR Sup. LEXIS 341 (1994).

Associated Press (2003, March 15). House approves voucher-type bill for schooling. *The Fort Collins Coloradoan.* Retrieved February 25, 2006, from www.coloradoan.com/news/coloradoanpublishing/government/legislature/031503_schoolvouchers.html.

Averett, N., and Wilkerson, J. E. (2002, August 4). Tax law little aid to poor students. *The Morning Call.*

Bagley v. Raymond School Department, 728 A.2d 127 (Me., 1999).

Baker v. Carr, 369 U.S. 186 (1962).

Barber, B. (1997). Public schooling: education for democracy. In *The Public Purpose of Education and Schooling,* ed. John I. Goodlad and Timothy J. McMannon. San Francisco: Jossey-Bass Publishers.

Barnard, J., Frangakis, C., Hill, J., and Rubin, D. (2003). Principal stratification approach to broken randomized experiments: A case study of school choice vouchers in New York City (with discussion). *Journal of the American Statistical Association* 98:299–323.

Barnett, W. S. (2002). Early childhood education. In *School reform proposals: The research evidence,* ed. Alex Molnar, 1–24. Greenwich, CT: Information Age Publishing.

Barrow, B. (2008, June 18). Voucher bill wins final legislative passage. *Nola.com* [*Times-Picayune*]. Retrieved June 19, 2008, from www.nola.com/news/index.ssf/2008/06/voucher_bill_wins_final_passag.html

Belfield, C. R. (2001). *Tuition tax credits: What do we know so far?* Occasional paper No. 33. National Center for the Study of Privatization in Education. Teachers College, Columbia University. Retrieved November 24, 2007, from www.ncspe.org/publications_files/530_OP33.pdf.

Belfield, C. R., and Levin, H. M. (2002). The effects of competition between schools on educational outcomes: A review for the United States. *Review of Educational Research* 72:279–341.

Betts, J. R., Rice, L. A., Zau, A. C., Tang, Y. E., and Koedel, C. R. (2006). *Does school choice work? Effects on student integration and achievement.* San Francisco: Public Policy Inst. of California.

Bifulco, R., and Ladd, H. (2006). *School choice, racial segregation and test-score gaps: Evidence from North Carolina's Charter School Program.* Paper presented at annual meeting of Allied Social Science Associations, Boston, MA, January 8, 2006.

Bittker, B. I. (1972). Charitable contributions: Tax deductions or matching grants? *Tax Law Review* 28(37):58–59.

Bland, K. (2000, April 9). School tax credits wide open to abuse. *The Arizona Republic,* p. A22.

Board of Education v. Allen, 392 U.S. 236 (1968).

Boaz, D., and Barrett, R. M. (1996). *What would a school voucher buy? The real cost of private schools.* Cato Institute, Briefing Paper No. 25. Washington DC: Cato

Institute. Retrieved February 22, 2006, from www.cato.org/pubs/briefs/bp-025 .html.

Booker, K., Zimmer, R., and Buddin, R. (2005). *The effect of charter schools on school peer composition.* Working Paper. Santa Monica, CA: RAND.

Bracey, G. W. (2003). The 13th Bracey Report on the Condition of Public Education. *Phi Delta Kappan* 85(2):148–164.

Brantlinger, P. (1983). *Bread and circuses: Theories of mass culture as social decay.* Ithaca, NY: Cornell University Press.

Braun, H., Jenkins, F., and Grigg, W. (2006). *Comparing private schools and public schools using hierarchical linear modeling.* U.S. Department of Education, Institute of Education Sciences, National Center for Education Statistics, NCES 2006-461.

Brown v. Board of Education, 347 U.S. 483 (1954).

Buddin, R. J., Cordes, J. J., and Kirby, S. N. (1998). School choice in California: Who chooses private schools? *Journal of Urban Economics* 44:110–34.

Burman, L. E. (2003). Is the tax expenditure concept still relevant? *National Tax Journal* 56:613–27.

Bush, G. W. (2002, July 1). *Speech in Cleveland.* Retrieved November 24, 2007, from www .whitehouse.gov/news/releases/2002/07/20020701-7.html.

Bush, J. (2007, November 10). An interview with Governor Jeb Bush, conducted by Michael Camarda. *The Politic.org.* Retrieved November 11, 2007, from thepolitic.org/ index.php?option=com_content&task=view&id=74&Itemid=0.

Bush v. Holmes, 867 So. 2d 1270 [Florida] (2004).

Bush v. Holmes, 919 So. 2d 392 [Florida] (2006).

Business Journal of Phoenix (2004, April 2). *Tuition tax credit gets kudos.* American City Business Journals, Inc.

Cain v. Horne, 2008 Ariz. App. LEXIS 77 [Arizona] (2008).

Camilli, G., and Bulkley, K. (2001). Critique of "An Evaluation of the Florida A-Plus Accountability and School Choice Program." *Education Policy Analysis Archives* 9(7). Retrieved November 24, 2007, from epaa.asu.edu/epaa/v9n7/.

Carnoy, M. (2002). *School vouchers: Examining the evidence.* Washington DC: Economic Policy Institute.

Carr, M., and Ritter, G. (2007). *Measuring the competitive effect of charter schools on student achievement in Ohio's traditional public schools.* Research Publication Series, National Center for the Study of Privatization in Education, Teachers College, Columbia University. Retrieved November 24, 2007, from www.ncspe.org/ publications_files/OP146.pdf.

Carter, S. (1993). *The culture of disbelief: How American law and politics trivialize religious devotion.* New York: Basic Books.

Catterall, J. S. (1983). *Tuition tax credits: Fact and fiction.* Bloomington, IN: Phi Delta Kappa Educational Foundation.

Chakrabarti, R. (2008). Can increasing private school participation and monetary loss in a voucher program affect public school performance? Evidence from Milwaukee. *Journal of Public Economics* 92(5–6):1371–1393.

Chittenden Town School District v. Department of Education, 169 Vt. 310, 738 A.2d 539 (1999).

Chubb, J. E., and Moe, T. M. (1990). *Politics, markets, and America's schools.* Washington DC: Brookings Institution Press.

Church of Lukumi Babalu Aye v. City of Hialeah, 508 U.S. 520 (1993).

Cobb, C., and Glass, G. (1999). Ethnic segregation in Arizona charter schools. *Education Policy Analysis Archives* 7(1). Retrieved November 24, 2007, from epaa.asu. edu/epaa/v7n1.

Collins Center for Public Policy (2002). *The Florida Corporate Income Tax Credit Scholarship Program: A preliminary analysis.* Tallahassee, FL: Collins Center for Public Policy.

Committee for Public Education v. Nyquist, 413 U.S. 756 (1973).

Committee for Public Education & Religious Liberty v. Regan, 444 U.S. 646 (1980).

Coons, J., and Sugarman, S. (1978). *Education by choice: The case for family control.* Berkeley: University of California Press.

County of Allegheny v. ACLU, 492 U.S. 573 (1989).

Cullen, Julie Berry, Jacob, Brian A., and Levitt, Steven D. (2005). "The impact of school choice on student outcomes: An analysis of the Chicago Public Schools." *Journal of Public Economics* 89(5-6):729–60.

Cullen, Julie Berry, Jacob, Brian A., and Levitt, Steven D. (2006). "The effect of school choice on participants: Evidence from randomized lotteries." *Econometrica* 74(5):1191–230.

Darling-Hammond, L. (2000). Teacher quality and student achievement: A review of state policy evidence. *Education Policy Analysis Archives* 8(1). Retrieved November 24, 2007, from epaa.asu.edu/epaa/v8n1/.

Darling-Hammond, L., et al. (1996). *What matters most: Teaching for America's future.* New York: National Commission on Teaching and America's Future.

Darling-Hammond, L., and Kirby, S. N. (1985). *Tuition tax deductions and parent school choice: A case study of Minnesota.* Santa Monica, CA: Rand.

Dáte, S. V. (2007, April 13). Appeals court throws out '05 conviction of voucher fraud. *Palm Beach Post.*

Davenport, P. (2008, May 15). 2 school voucher programs overturned as unconstitutional. Fox11Az.com. Retrieved May 24, 2008, from www.fox11az.com/news/topstories/stories/tucson-20080515-voucher-programs-unconstitutional.1044086a7.html.

Davey v. Locke, 299 F.3d 748 (9th Cir., 2002).

Dolinski, C. (2008, April 25). Panel to put school vouchers on November ballot. *Tampa Bay Tribune.* Retrieved April 26, 2008, from www2.tbo.com/content/2008/apr/25/state-panel-opts-ask-voters-vote-voucher-change.

Ducasse, R. (2005, December 8). Personal conversation with author.

DuPont, P. (2002, July 31). Blaine is slain. *Wall Street Journal (Opinion Journal).* Available online at www.opinionjournal.com/columnists/pdupont/?id=110002060.

Editors (2004, November 30). Words instead of action. Editorial, *Daytona Beach News-Journal.*

Employment Division v. Smith, 494 U.S. 872 (1990).

Enlow, R. C. (2004). Grading vouchers: Ranking America's top school choice programs. *School Choice Issues in Depth* 2(1). Indianapolis, IN: Milton and Rose D. Friedman Foundation.

Enlow, R. (2008). *The ABCs of school choice.* Indianapolis, IN: Milton and Rose D. Friedman Foundation.

Erdley, D. (2002a, March 24). Pennsylvania plan may be best in nation. *Pittsburgh Tribune-Review.*

———. (2002b, March 24). State tax credit a bonanza to private education. *Pittsburgh Tribune-Review.*

———. (2004, June 21). Critics say tax credit plan needs checks. *Pittsburgh Tribune-Review.* Retrieved February 24, 2006, from www.pittsburghlive.com/x/tribune-review/trib/pittsburgh/s_199753.html.

Everson v. Board of Education of the Township of Ewing, 330 U.S. 1 (1947).

Fairlie, R. W. (2006). *Racial segregation and the private/public school choice.* Research Publication Series, National Center for the Study of Privatization in Education, Teachers College, Columbia University. Retrieved November 24, 2007, from www.ncspe.org/publications_files/OP124.pdf.

Feldman, S. (1997). *Let's tell the truth.* Washington DC. American Federation of Teachers. Retrieved November 24, 2007, from www.aft.org/presscenter/speeches-columns/wws/1997/1197.htm.

Figlio, D. N., and Rouse, C. E. (2006). Do accountability and voucher threats improve low-performing schools? *Journal of Public Economics* 90(1–2):239–55.

Finn, J. D., Gerber, S. B., Achilles, C. M., and Boyd-Zaharias, J. (2001). The enduring effects of small classes. *Teachers College Record* 103(2):145–83.

Fiske, E. B., and Ladd, H. F. (2000). *When schools compete: A cautionary tale.* Washington DC: The Brookings Institution Press.

FloridaChild (undated). *FloridaChild Scholarships: Information for Corporations.* Retrieved November 3, 2007, from www.floridachild.com/scholarships/scholarships corp.html.

Florida Department of Education (2007a). *Corporate tax credit scholarship program.* Retrieved November 23, 2007, from www.floridaschoolchoice.org/Information/CTC/files/ctc_fast_facts.pdf.

———. (2007b). *Corporate tax credit scholarship program, November [2007] quarterly report.* Retrieved November 23, 2007, from www.floridaschoolchoice.org/Information/CTC/quarterly_reports/ctc_report_nov2007.pdf.

———. (2007c). *OSP Eligibility Requirements.* Retrieved November 24, 2007, from www.floridaschoolchoice.org/Information/OSP/eligibility.asp.

Florida Senate Committee on Education (2003). *Corporate tax credit scholarship program accountability.* Interim Project Report 2004-132. Tallahassee: Florida Senate Committee on Education.

Frankenberg, E., and Lee, C. (2003, September 5). Charter schools and race: A lost opportunity for integrated education. *Education Policy Analysis Archives* 11(32). Retrieved November 3, 2007, from epaa.asu.edu/epaa/v11n32/.

Friedman, M. (1955). The role of government in education. In *Economics and the public interest,* ed. Robert Solo, 127–34. New Brunswick, NJ: Rutgers University Press.

———. (1962). *Capitalism and freedom*. Chicago: University of Chicago Press.

Fuller, B., Elmore, R., and Orfield, G. (1996). *Who chooses? Who loses?: Culture, institutions, and the unequal effects of school choice*. New York: Teachers College Press.

Gallagher, T. (2003). *Corporate Tax Credit Scholarship Program*. Tallahassee, FL: Department of Financial Services.

Galston, W. (1991). *Liberal purposes: Goods, virtues, and diversity in the liberal state*. Cambridge: Cambridge University Press.

Gehrke, R. (2007, November 14). Voucher defeat may cost Utah Republicans in '08 polls. *The Salt Lake Tribune*.

General Accounting Office. (2001). *School vouchers: Publicly funded programs in Cleveland and Milwaukee*. Washington DC: GAO.

———. (2002). *School vouchers: Characteristics of privately funded programs*. Washington DC: GAO.

Genier v. McNulty, No. 03-CV-96 (D. Vt.), filed in federal district court in Vermont on March 21, 2003 (described in a press release available online). Retrieved November 3, 2007, from www.schoolreport.com/ij_press_release_3_03.htm#background.

Gill, B. P., Timpane, P. M., Ross, K. E., Brewer, D. J., and Booker, K. (2007). *Rhetoric vs. reality: What we know and what we need to know about vouchers and charter schools*. Santa Monica, CA: RAND. Retrieved November 3, 2007, from www.rand.org/pubs/monograph_reports/2007/RAND_MR1118-1.pdf.

Good News Club v. Milford Central School, 533 U.S. 98 (2001).

Goodstein, L. (2002, June 30). In states, hurdles loom, *New York Times*, Section 4, Page 3.

Gottlob, B. (2004). *The fiscal impacts of school choice in New Hampshire*. Indianapolis, IN: The Josiah Bartlett Center for Public Policy and the Milton and Rose D. Friedman Foundation.

———. (2007). *The high cost of low graduation rates in North Carolina*. Indianapolis, IN: The Milton and Rose D. Friedman Foundation.

Government Accountability Office (2005). *Understanding the tax reform debate: Background, criteria, & questions*. (GAO-05-1009SP) Washington DC: GAO.

Green v. School Board of New Kent County, 391 US 430 (1968).

Greene, J. P. (2001). *An evaluation of the Florida A-Plus Accountability and School Choice Program*. New York: The Manhattan Institute.

Greene, J. P., Howell, W., and Peterson, P. (1998). Lessons from the Cleveland Scholarship Program. In *Learning from School Choice*, 357–92. Washington DC: Brookings Institution Press.

———. (1999). *An evaluation of the Cleveland voucher program after two years*. Cambridge, MA: Program on Education Policy and Governance, Harvard University.

Greene, J. P., Peterson, P., and Du, J. (1996). *The effectiveness of school choice in Milwaukee: A secondary analysis of data from the program's evaluation*. Cambridge, MA: Harvard University, John F. Kennedy School of Government.

———. (1997). *Effectiveness of school choice: The Milwaukee experiment*. Cambridge, MA: Harvard University.

———. (1998). School choice in Milwaukee: A randomized experiment. In *Learning from School Choice*, 335–356. Washington DC: Brookings Institution Press.

Greene, J. P., and Winters, M. (2003). *When schools compete: The effects of vouchers on Florida public school achievement.* New York: The Manhattan Institute.

———. (2008). *The effect of special education vouchers on public school achievement: Evidence from Florida's Mckay Scholarship program.* New York: The Manhattan Institute.

Griffith v. Bower, 319 Ill. App. 3d 993 (5th Dist.), *app. denied*, 195 Ill. 2d 577 (2001).

Peter D. Hart Research Associates. (1998). *Public attitudes on school choice and vouchers.* Washington DC: Peter D. Hart Research Associates.

Hastings, J., Kane, T., and Staiger, D. (2005). *Parental preferences and school competition: Evidence from a public school choice program.* Working paper. Cambridge, MA: National Bureau of Economic Research.

Herzberg, R. Q., and Fawson, C. (2004). *Estimating demand and supply response to tuition tax credits for private school tuition in Utah.* Logan, UT: Utah State University.

Hess, F. (2002). *Revolution at the margins: The impact of competition on urban school systems.* Washington DC: Brookings Institution Press.

Hibbs v. Winn, 542 U.S. 88 (2004).

Hibbs v. Winn, 361 F.Supp.2d 1117 (2005).

Hill, P. T. (2007, September 7). Waiting for the "tipping point": Why school choice is proving to be so hard. *Education Week* 27(2):26–27.

Home School Legal Defense Association [HSLDA] (2004, August 19). *Why are educational tax credits important?* Purcellville, VA: HSLDA. Retrieved September 29, 2005, from www.hslda.org/docs/nche/000010/200308190.asp.

Howe, K. R. (1997). *Understanding equal educational opportunity: Social justice, democracy, and schooling.* New York: Teachers College Press.

Howe, K., Eisenhart, M., and Betebenner, D. (2001, October). School choice crucible: A case study of Boulder Valley. *Phi Delta Kappan* 83(2):137–46.

Howe, K., and Welner, K. (2002). School choice and the pressure to perform: Déjà vu for children with disabilities? *Journal of Remedial and Special Education* 23(4):212–21.

Howell, W. (2002). The data vacuum. *Education next* 2(2):79–83.

Howell, W. G., and Peterson, P. E. (2000). *School choice in Dayton, Ohio: An evaluation after one year.* Paper presented at the Conference on Vouchers, Charters and Public Education sponsored by the Program on Education Policy and Governance, Harvard University, Cambridge, MA.

Howell, W. G., Peterson, P. E., Wolf, P., and Campbell, D. E. (2002). *The education gap: vouchers and urban schools.* Washington DC: Brookings Institution Press.

Howell, W. G., Wolf, P., Campbell, D. E., and Peterson, P. E. (2002). School vouchers and academic performance: Results from three randomized field trials. *Journal of Policy Analysis and Management* 21(2):191–217.

Hoxby, C. (2002). How school choice affects the achievement of public school students. In *Choice with equity*, ed. Paul Hill. Stanford, CA: Hoover Institution Press.

———. (2003a). School choice and school competition: Evidence from the United States. *Swedish Economic Policy Review* 10:11–67.

———. (2003b). School choice and school productivity (or, could school choice be a tide that lifts all boats?). In *The economics of school choice*, ed. C. Hoxby. Chicago: University of Chicago Press.

Hoxby, C., and Murarka, S. (2006). Comprehensive yet simple: Florida's tapestry of school choice programs. In *Reforming education in Florida: A study prepared by the Koret Task Force on K-12 education*, ed. Paul E. Peterson, 167–211. Stanford, CA: Hoover Institution Press.

Hsieh, C., and Urquiola, M. (2003). *When schools compete, how do they compete? An assessment of Chile's nationwide school voucher program.* NBER Working Paper No. 10008.

Huerta, L. A., and d'Entremont, C. (2007). Education tax credits in a post-*Zelman* era: Legal, political, and policy alternatives to vouchers? *Education Policy* 21(1), 73–109.

Jackson v. Benson, 578 N.W.2d 602 (Wisc.), *cert. denied*, 525 U.S. 997 (1998).

James, T., and Levin, H. M., eds. (1983). *Public dollars for private schools: The case of tuition tax credits.* Philadelphia, PA: Temple University Press.

Keegan, L. G. (2001, December 18). *Tuition tax credits: A model for school choice (No. 384).* Washington DC: National Center for Policy Analysis.

Kemerer, F. R. (1998). The constitutional dimension of school vouchers. *Texas Forum on Civil Liberties & Civil Rights* 3:137.

Klas, M. E. (2006, May 5). Vouchers saved, but Bush won't get amendment. *Miami Herald.*

Kossan, P. (2002, March 23). School tax credits fail poor. *The Arizona Republic.*

———. (2007, October 2). Tax credit leaves room for misuse. *The Arizona Republic.*

———. (2008, July 1). State court OKs school vouchers. *The Arizona Republic.*

Kotterman v. Killian, 972 P.2d 606 [Arizona] (1999).

Krueger, A., and Whitmore, D. (2002). Would smaller classes help close the black-white achievement gap? In *Bridging the achievement gap*, ed. John Chubb and Tom Loveless, 11–46. Washington DC: Brookings Institute Press.

Krueger, A., and Zhu, P. (2004). Another look at the New York City school voucher experiment. *American Behavioral Scientist* 47(5):658–98.

Kupermintz, H. (2001). The effects of vouchers on school improvement: Another look at the Florida data. *Education Policy Analysis Archives* 9(8). Retrieved November 24, 2007, from epaa.asu.edu/epaa/v9n8/.

Lacireno-Paquet, N., and Brantley, C. (2008). *What do we know about the characteristics and motivations of families who actively choose schools?* Tempe, AZ, and Boulder, CO: Educational Policy Research Unit and Education and the Public Interest Center.

Ladd, H. (2003). *School vouchers and student achievement: What we know so far.* Policy Brief, Center for the Child and Family Policy 2(1). Durham, NC: Duke University.

Ladd, H., and Glennie, E. (2001). Appendix C: A replication of Jay Greene's voucher effect study using North Carolina data. In *School vouchers: Examining the evidence*, ed. M. Carnoy. Washington DC: Economic Policy Institute.

Lakoff, G. (2004). *Don't think of an elephant! Know your values and frame the debate.* White River Junction, VT: Chelsea Green Publishing Company.

Lamb's Chapel v. Center Moriches Union Free School District, 508 U.S. 384 (1993).

Lamer, T. (2006, May 20). Fighting on better ground. *World Magazine* 21(20). Retrieved September 5, 2007, from www.worldmag.com/articles/11863.

Lankford, H., and Wyckoff, J. (2001). Who would be left behind by enhanced private school choice? *Journal of Urban Economics* 50(2):288–312.

———. (2005). Why are schools racially segregated? Implications for school choice policies. In *School choice and diversity: What the evidence says*, ed. J. Scott, 9–26. Teachers College Press.

LeFevre, A. (2005, September 1). Pennsylvania expands tax credit program. *School Reform News*. The Heartland Institute.

———. (2006, March 6). School choice can save tax dollars. *The Patriot News*.

Lemon v. Kurtzman, 403 U.S. 602 (1971).

Lindsay, C. (2004). *Fiscal impact of the Universal Scholarship Tax Credit Proposal.* Clemson University, South Carolina Policy Council and the LEAD Foundation.

Lips, C., and Jacoby, J. (2001, September 17). *The Arizona education tax credit: Giving parents choices, saving taxpayers money. No. 414.* Washington DC: Cato Institute.

Locke v. Davey, 540 U.S. 712 (2004).

Lubienski, C. (2005). Public schools in marketized environments: Shifting incentives and unintended consequences of competition based educational reforms. *American Journal of Education* 111(4):464–86.

Lubienski, C., and Gulosino, C. (2007). *Choice, competition, and organizational orientation: A geo-spatial analysis of charter schools and the distribution of educational opportunities* (Occasional Paper No. 148). New York: National Center for the Study of Privatization in Education, Teachers College, Columbia University.

Lubienski, C., and Lubienski, S. T. (2006a). *Charter, private, public schools and academic achievement: New evidence from NAEP mathematics data.* New York: Teachers College Columbia, National Center for the Study of Privatization in Education. Retrieved June 18, 2006, from http://www.ncspe.org/publications_files/OP111.pdf.

———. (2006b). Review of "On the Public-Private School Achievement Debate." Tempe, AZ: Educational Policy Research Unit. Retrieved November 18, 2007, from epsl.asu.edu/epru/ttreviews/EPSL-0608-207-EPRU.pdf.

Lubienski, C., Crane, C., and Lubienski, S. T. (2008). What do we know about school effectiveness? Academic gains in public and private schools. *Phi Delta Kappan* 89(9):689–695.

Lukas, C. L. (2003, December 11). The Arizona Scholarship Tax Credit: Providing choice for Arizona taxpayers and students. *Policy Report No. 186.* Phoenix, AZ: Goldwater Institute.

Lupu, I. C., and Tuttle, R. W. (2003). Zelman's future: Vouchers, sectarian providers, and the next round of constitutional battles. *Notre Dame L. Rev.* 78:917.

Luthens v. Bair, 788 F. Supp. 1032 (S.D. Iowa 1992).

Lynch v. Donnelly, 465 U.S. 668 (1984).

Macedo, S. (2000). *Diversity and distrust: Civic education in a multicultural democracy.* Cambridge: Harvard University Press.

Madison, J. (1778). *The Federalist Papers No. 45: The Alleged Danger from the Powers of the Union to the State Governments Considered.*

Mann, H. (1891 [1848]). Twelfth annual report for 1848 of the Secretary of the Board of Education of Massachusetts. In *Life and works of Horace Mann,* ed. M. Mann, vol. 4, 222–340. Boston: Lee and Shepard Publishers.

Mathematica (2003). *New York City school choice: Rigorous evidence informs the debate.* Retrieved November 24, 2007, from www.mathematica-mpr.com/education/school.asp.

Mator, A. (2006, May 20). Credit worthy. *World Magazine* 21(20). Retrieved September 5, 2007, from www.worldmag.com/articles/11863.

Mayer, D. P., Peterson, P. E., Myers, D., Tuttle, C. C., and Howell, W. G. (2002). *School choice in New York City after three years: An evaluation of the School Choice Scholarships Program.* Washington DC: Mathematica Policy Research. Retrieved November 24, 2007, from www.mathematica-mpr.com/publications/PDFs/nycfull.pdf.

McCulloch v. Maryland, 17 U.S. (4 Wheat.) 316 (1819).

McCutchen, K. (2008, May 16). School choice advances in Georgia. *The Daily Citizen.* Retrieved May 16, 2008, from www.northwestgeorgia.com/opinion/local_story_137124851.html.

McDaniel v. Paty, 435 U.S. 618 (1978).

McEwan, P. J. (2004). The potential impact of vouchers. *Peabody Journal of Education* 79:57–80.

McEwan, P. J., and Carnoy, M. (2000). The effectiveness and efficiency of private schools in Chile's voucher system. *Educational Evaluation and Policy Analysis* 22:213–39.

McNeil, M. (2008, May 8). Conservatives are abandoning vouchers? Seriously? *Education Week,* Campaign K-12 blog. Retrieved May 25, 2008, from blogs.edweek.org/edweek/campaign-k-12/2008/05/conservatives_are_abandoning_v.html.

Meek v. Pittenger, 421 U.S. 349 (1975).

Metcalf, K. K. (1999). *Evaluation of the Cleveland Scholarship and Tutoring Grant Program, 1996–1999.* Bloomington: The Indiana Center for Evaluation, Indiana University.

———. (2001). *Evaluation of the Cleveland Scholarship and Tutoring Program, 1998–2000: Technical Report.* Bloomington: Indiana Center for Evaluation, Indiana University.

Metcalf, K. K., and Legan, N. A. (2006). Interpreting voucher research: The influence of multiple comparison groups and types. *Journal of School Choice: Research, Theory, and Practice* 1(1): 47–64.

Metcalf, K. K., et al. (1998a). *A comparative evaluation of the Cleveland Scholarship and Tutoring Grant Program, year one: 1996–97.* Bloomington: School of Education, Indiana University.

———. (1998b). *Evaluation of the Cleveland Scholarship and Tutoring Program: Second year report (1997–98).* Bloomington: The Indiana Center for Evaluation, Indiana University.

———. (2001). *Evaluation of the Cleveland Scholarship and Tutoring Grant Program.* Bloomington: Indiana University, Indiana Center for Evaluation.

———. (2003a). *Evaluation of the Cleveland Scholarship and Tutoring Program, 1998–2001: Technical report.* Bloomington: Indiana Center for Evaluation, Indiana University.

———. (2003b). *Evaluation of the Cleveland Scholarship and Tutoring Program, 1998–2002: Technical report.* Bloomington: Indiana Center for Evaluation, Indiana University.

Miller, K. (2006a, April 28). Voucher controls within reach after 2 years of slipping away. *Palm Beach Post.*

———. (2006b, May 5). Legislature OKs oversight of vouchers. *Palm Beach Post.*

Miron, G., and Nelson, C. (2002). *What's public about charter schools: Lessons learned about school choice and accountability.* Thousand Oaks, CA: Corwin Press.

Mitchell v. Helms, 530 U.S. 793 (2000).

Molnar, A. (1997, August 6). The real lesson of Milwaukee's voucher experiment. *Education Week* 16.

Moore, W. A. (2008, February 1). Health agency scandal growing. *St. Petersburg Times.*

Mueller v. Allen, 463 U.S. 388 (1983).

Muraskin, L. (1998). *Barriers, benefits, and costs of using private schools to alleviate overcrowding in public schools.* U.S. Department of Education. Planning and Evaluation Service.

Murphy, J. (2007, April 5). Smith offers alternative to Rendell on education. *The Patriot News.*

Myers, D., Peterson, P. E., Chou, J., and Howell, W. G. (2000). *School choice in New York City after two years: An evaluation of the school choice scholarships program.* Washington DC: Mathematica Policy Research.

National Commission on Teaching and America's Future (2004). *Fifty years after Brown: A two-tiered educational system.* Washington DC: National Commission on Teaching and America's Future.

National Working Commission on Choice in K-12 Education (2003). *School choice: Doing it the right way makes a difference.* Washington DC: The Brown Center on Education Policy, The Brookings Institution.

Nelson, F., Van Meter, N., Muir, E., and Drown, R. (2001). Public money and privatization in K-12 education. In *Education Finance in the New Millennium* (Yearbook of the American Education Finance Association), ed. S. Chaikind and W. Fowler, 173–88. Larchmont, NY: Eye on Education.

Oakes, J. (1985). *Keeping track: How schools structure inequality.* New Haven, CT: Yale University Press.

———. (2005). *Keeping track: How schools structure inequality.* (2nd edition). New Haven, CT: Yale University Press.

Oakes, J., Quartz, K. H., Ryan, S., and Lipton, M. (1999). *Becoming good American schools: The struggle for civic virtue in education reform.* San Francisco: Jossey-Bass Publishers.

O'Day, J. (2002). Complexity, accountability, and school improvement. *Harvard Educational Review* 72(3): 293–329.

Omand, H. L. (2003, November 6). Vacuous vouchers: Tax credits deliver genuine school choice. *National Review Online.* Retrieved September 3, 2007, from www.nationalreview.com/nrof_comment/omand200311060851.asp.

Opinion of the Justices to the Senate, 401 Mass. 1201, 514 N.E.2d 353 (1987).

Owens v. Colorado Congress of Parents, 92 P.3d 933 [Colorado] (2004).

Paige, R. (2002, June 28). A win for America's children. *The Washington Post,* p. A29.

People for the American Way (2003). *Community voice or captive of the right? A closer look at the black alliance for educational options.* Washington DC: People for the American Way.

Peterson, P. E. (2001). This just in: Vouchers work. *Hoover Digest* 2001(3). Palo Alto, CA: Hoover Institution. Retrieved November 24, 2007, from www.hoover.org/publications/digest/3459396.html.

Peterson, P. E., Greene J. P., Howell, W. G., and McCready, W. (1998). *Initial findings from an evaluation of school choice programs in Washington, D.C. and Dayton, Ohio.* Paper presented at the annual meeting of the Association of Public Policy and Management, New York, NY.

Peterson, P. E., and Llaudet, E. (2006). *On the public-private school achievement debate.* (No. PEPG 06-02). Cambridge, MA: Program on Education Policy and Governance, Harvard University.

Peterson, P. E., Myers, D., Haimson, J., and Howell, W. G. (1997). *Initial findings from the evaluation of the New York School Choice Scholarships Program.* Washington DC: Mathematica Policy Research.

Peterson, P. E., Myers, D., and Howell, W. G. (1998). *An evaluation of the New York City School Choice Scholarships Program: The first year.* Washington DC: Mathematica Policy Research.

Ravitch, D. (2001, October 8). Why liberals should be pro-choice. *New Republic,* pp. 31–38.

REACH Foundation (n.d.). *How many children have received scholarships through the EITC program?* Retrieved November 24, 2007, from www.paschoolchoice.org/reach/cwp/view.asp?A=1368&Q=568683.

———. *Sample computations for "C" corporations participating in the Educational Improvement Tax Credit.* Retrieved June 17, 2006, from www.paschoolchoice.org/reach/cwp/view.asp?a=1367&q=56.

Ready, D., Lee, V., and Welner, K. G. (2004). Educational equity and school structure: School size, overcrowding, and schools-within-schools. *Teachers College Record* 106(10):1989–2014.

Reynolds v. United States, 98 U.S. 145 (1879).

Reynolds, A. J., Temple, J. A., Robertson, D. L., and Mann, E. A. (2001). Longterm effects of an early childhood intervention on educational achievement and juvenile arrest: A 15-year follow-up of low-income children in public schools. *Journal of the American Medical Association* 285(18):2339–46.

Richard, A. (2004, February 4). Florida school choice group leaves scholarship program. *Education Week* 23(21):17.

Richards, J. S. (2006, June 7). Vouchers abused, state says. *Columbus Dispatch.*

Robelen, E. (2008, May 7). Iowa mandates "core curriculum" for private schools. *Education Week* 27(36):11.

Robinson, A. (2000). Risky credit: Tuition tax credits and issues of accountability and equity. *Stanford Law & Policy Review* 11:253.

Roman, I. (2000, March 24). School-voucher fund likely to be killed in Puerto Rico. *The Orlando Sentinel.* Retrieved February 18, 2006, from www.puertorico-herald .org/issues/vol4n13/vouchers-en.shtml.

Romer v. Evans, 517 U.S. 620 (1996).

Rosenberger v. Rector & Visitors, 515 U.S. 819 (1995).

Rothstein. L. (1999). School choice and students with disabilities. In *School choice and social controversy: Politics, policy, & law,* ed. S. Sugarman and F. Kremerer, 332–64. Washington DC: Brookings Institution Press.

Rouse, C. E. (1998). Private school vouchers and student achievement: An evaluation of the Milwaukee parental choice program. *The Quarterly Journal of Economics* 113(2).

———. (2000). *School reform in the 21st century: A look at the effect of class size and school vouchers on the academic achievement of minority students,* working paper #440, Industrial Relations Section, Princeton University. Retrieved November 24, 2007, from www.irs.princeton.edu/pubs/pdfs/440.pdf.

Rouse, C. E., Hannaway, J., Goldhaber, D., and Figlio, D. (2007) *Feeling the Florida heat?: How low-performing schools respond to voucher and accountability pressure* (CALDER Working Paper 13). Retrieved December 7, 2007, from www.caldercenter .org/PDF/1001116_Florida_Heat.pdf.

Rust v. Sullivan, 500 U.S. 173 (1991).

Saporito, S., and Sohoni, D. (2006). Coloring outside the lines: Racial segregation in public schools and their attendance boundaries, *Sociology of Education* 79:81–105.

Sawhill, I., and Smith, S. (2000). Vouchers for elementary and secondary education. In *Vouchers and the provision ofpublic services,* ed. Eugene Steuerle, et al. Washington DC: Brookings Institution Press.

Schaeffer, A. B. (2007). *The Public Education Tax Credit.* Policy Analysis No. 605. Washington DC: Cato Institute. Retrieved December 7, 2007, from www.cato.org/ pubs/pas/pa-605.pdf.

School Choice Wisconsin (2005). *Enrollment Growth* [Cleveland]. Retrieved November 24, 2007, from www.schoolchoiceinfo.org/facts/index.cfm?fpt_id=5&fl_id=2.

Schwartz, B. (2004). *The paradox of choice: Why more is less.* New York: Ecco.

Schwartz, B., Markus, H. R., and Snibbe, A. C. (2006, February 26). Is freedom just another word for many things to buy? *New York Times Magazine,* p. 14.

Schwartz, R. M., Askew, B. J., and Gómez-Bellengé, F. X. (2007). *What works? Reading recovery: An analysis of the What Works Clearinghouse Intervention Report issued March 19, 2007.* Worthington, OH: Reading Recovery Council of North America.

Scutari, C. (2006, March 30). Corporate tuition tax credit is law. *The Arizona Republic.*

Sherwood, R. (2006, June 17). Budget on way. *The Arizona Republic.*

Simmons-Harris v. Goff, 711 N.E.2d 203 (Ohio, 1999).

Smole, D. P. (2003). *School choice: Current legislation.* Washington DC: Congressional Research Service.

Smrekar, C., and Goldring, E. (1999). *School choice in urban America: Magnet schools and the pursuit of equity.* New York: Teachers College Press.

Snell, L. (2002, April 2). Arizona Tax-Credit Program: Successful example of a school-choice initiative. *Reason Foundation Policy Update* 18. Los Angeles: The Reason Foundation.

Soifer, D. (2006, June 1). *Federal tuition tax credit proposals gather steam on Capitol Hill.* Chicago: The Heartland Institute. Retrieved November 23, 2007, from www.heartland.org/Article.cfm?artId=19162.

St. Petersburg Times Editorial Board (2006, May 9). A dubious virtual voucher. *St. Petersburg Times.*

Stone v. Graham, 449 U.S. 39 (1980).

Strauss, V., and Turque, B. (2008, June 9). Fate of D.C. voucher program darkens. *Washington Post*, p. B01.

Surrey, S. S. (1970). Tax incentives as a device for implementing government policy: A comparison with direct government expenditures. *Harvard Law Review* 83:705.

Surrey, S. S., and McDaniel, P. R. (1985). *Tax expenditures.* Cambridge, MA: Harvard University Press.

Sykes, G., and Plank, D. (2003). *Choosing choice: School choice in international perspective.* New York: Teachers College Press.

Tannen, D. (2003, September 1). Let them eat words. *The American Prospect* 14(8):29–31.

Teske, P., and Reichardt, R. (2006). Doing their homework: How charter school parents make their choices. In *Hopes, fears and realities: A balanced look at American charter schools in 2006*, ed. R. J. Lake and P. T. Hill, 1–9. Seattle: University of Washington. Retrieved November 24, 2007, from www.ncsrp.org/cs/csr/download/csr_files/HFR06_Chap1.pdf.

Teske, P., and Schneider, M. (2001). What research can tell policymakers about school choice. *Journal of Policy Analysis and Management* 20(4):609–31.

Teske, P., Schneider, M., Buckley, J., and Clark, S. (2000). *Does charter school competition improve traditional public schools?* New York: Manhattan Institute.

Tierney, J. (2006, March 7). City schools that work. *New York Times*, p. A21.

Toder, E. (1999). *The changing composition of tax incentives, 1980–99.* Washington DC: Urban Institute. Retrieved February 17, 2006, from http://www.urban.org/url.cfm?ID=410329.

Toney v. Bower, 318 Ill. App. 3d 1194 (4th Dist.), *app. denied*, 195 Ill. 2d 573 (2001).

Tropp, L. R., and Prenovost, M. A. (2008). The role of intergroup contact in predicting children's inter-ethnic attitudes: Evidence from meta-analytic and field studies. In *Intergroup relations: An integrative developmental and social psychological perspective*, ed. S. Levy and M. Killen. Oxford, England: Oxford University Press.

Turque, B. (2008, June 17). Voucher funds backed, with warning. *Washington Post*, p. B04.

United States Department of Education (2007). *Education options in the states: State programs that provide financial assistance for attendance at private elementary or secondary schools.* Washington DC: Office of Non-Public Education, Office of Innovation and Improvement.

Viteritti, J. P. (1996). Choosing equality: Religious freedom and educational opportunity under constitutional federalism. *Yale Law and Policy Review* 15:113.

———. (1999). *Choosing equality: School choice, the Constitution, and civil society.* Washington DC: Brookings Institution Press.

Wallace v. Jaffree, 472 U.S. 38 (1985).

Weiher, G. R., and Tedin, K. L. (2002). Does choice lead to racially distinctive schools? Charter schools and household preferences. *Journal of Policy Analysis and Management* 21(1):79–92.

Weiler, D. (1974). *Public school voucher demonstration: The first year at Alum Rock, summary and conclusions.* Santa Monica, CA: RAND.

Welner, K. G. (2000). Taxing the Establishment Clause: The revolutionary decision of the Arizona Supreme Court in Kotterman v. Killian. *Education Policy Analysis Archives* 8(36). Retrieved November 24, 2007, from epaa.asu.edu/epaa/v8n36.

———. (2002). *Peer analysis of proposal to expand educational scholarships.* Tempe, AZ: EPRU Policy Center. Retrieved November 24, 2007, from epsl.asu.edu/epru/peer_reviews/EPRU%202002-111/EPSL-0204-111-EPRU.doc.

———. (2003). *An examination of Colorado's tuition tax credit proposal.* Boulder, CO: EPIC Policy Center. Retrieved November 24, 2007, from epicpolicy.org/files/TaxCreditColoradoWelner.pdf.

———. (2004). *Colorado's voucher law. Examining the claim of fiscal neutrality. Education Policy Analysis Archives* 12(31). Retrieved November 24, 2007, from epaa.asu.edu/epaa/v12n31/.

Wenglinsky, H. (2007). *Are private high schools better academically than public high schools?* Washington DC: Center on Education Policy. Retrieved November 24, 2007, from www.cep-dc.org/index.cfm?fuseaction=document.showDocumentByID&nodeID=1&DocumentID=226.

West, M. R., and Peterson, P. E. (2006). The efficacy of choice threats within school accountability systems: Results from legislatively induced experiments. *Economic Journal* 116(510):C46–C62.

West, M. R., Peterson, P. E., and Campbell, D. E. (2001). *School choice in Dayton, Ohio after two years: An evaluation of the parents advancing choice in education scholarship program.* Cambridge, MA: Program on Education Policy and Governance, Harvard University.

Widmar v. Vincent, 454 U.S. 263 (1981).

Wilson, G. Y. (2002). *The equity impact of Arizona's education tax credit program: A review of the first three years (1998–2000).* Retrieved November 24, 2007, from www.asu.edu/educ/epsl/EPRU/documents/EPRU%202002-110/epru-0203-110.htm.

Winerip, M. (2003, May 7). What some much-noted data really showed about vouchers. *New York Times.*

Wisconsin Department of Public Instruction (2005). Milwaukee Parental Choice Program Homepage. Retrieved November 24, 2007, from dpi.wi.gov/sms/choice.html.

Wisconsin Legislative Audit Bureau (2000). *An evaluation: Milwaukee parental choice program (00-2).* Madison, WI: Wisconsin Legislative Audit Bureau.

Witte, J. F. (1997). *Achievement effects of the Milwaukee voucher program.* Paper presented at the 1997 American Economics Association Annual Meeting, New Orleans, LA.

———. (1998). The Milwaukee voucher experiment. *Educational Evaluation and Policy Analysis* 20(4):229–51.

———. (1999). School choice in action: The Milwaukee voucher program. *Civil Rights Law Journal* 10(1):1001–11.

———. (2000). *The market approach to education: An analysis of America's first voucher program*. Princeton, NJ: Princeton University Press.

Witte, J. F., Sterr, T. D., and Thorn, C. A. (1995). *Fifth year report, Milwaukee Parental Choice Program*. University of Wisconsin–Madison.

Witte, J. F., and Thorn, C. A. (1994). *Fourth year report, Milwaukee Parental Choice Program*. University of Wisconsin–Madison.

———. (1996). Who chooses? Vouchers and interdistrict choice programs in Milwaukee. *American Journal of Education* 104:186–217.

Witters v. Washington Department of Services for the Blind, 474 U.S. 481 (1986).

Wolf, P. J., and Hoople, D. S. (2006). Looking inside the black box: What school factors explain voucher gains in Washington DC? *Peabody Journal of Education* 81(1):7–26.

Wolf, P. J., Gutmann, B., Puma, M., Kisida, B., Rizzo, L., Eissa, N., and Silverberg, M. (2008). *Evaluation of the DC Opportunity Scholarship Program: Impacts after two years*. Washington DC: U.S. Department of Education, Institute of Education Studies.

Wolf, P. J., Gutmann, B., Puma, M., Rizzo, L., Eissa, N., and Silverberg, M. (2007). *Evaluation of the DC Opportunity Scholarship Program: Impacts after one year*. U.S. Department of Education, Institute of Education Sciences. Washington DC: U.S. Government Printing Office.

Wolf, P., Howell, W. G., and Peterson, P. E. (2000). *School choice in Washington, D.C.: An evaluation after one year*. Paper presented at the Conference on Vouchers, Charters and Public Education sponsored by the Program on Education Policy and Governance, Harvard University, Cambridge, MA.

Wolf, P., Peterson, P. E., and West, M. R. (2001). *Results of a school voucher experiment: The case of Washington, D.C., after two years*. Paper presented at the annual meeting of the American Political Science Association, San Francisco, CA.

Yettick, H., Love, E. W., and Anderson, S. (2008). Parental decision making and educational opportunity. In *Education policy and law: Current issues*, ed. Kevin Welner and Wendy Chi, 99–120. Greenwich, CT: Information Age Publishing.

Yun, J. T. (2008). *Review of "The effect of special education vouchers on public school achievement: Evidence from Florida's McKay Scholarship program."* Boulder and Tempe: Education and the Public Interest Center & Education Policy Research Unit. Retrieved May 24, 2008, from epicpolicy.org/thinktank/review-effect-of-special.

Zelman v. Simmons-Harris, 536 U.S. 639 (2002).

Zobrest v. Catalina Foothills School District, 509 U.S. 1 (1993).

Index

About the Author

Kevin G. Welner is associate professor of education in the educational foundations, policy, and practice program area. He is director of the University of Colorado at Boulder Education and the Public Interest Center (EPIC). Welner's present research examines issues concerning the intersection between education rights litigation and educational opportunity scholarship. His past research studied the change process associated with equity-minded reform efforts—reforms aimed at benefiting those who hold less powerful school and community positions (primarily Latinos, African Americans, and the poor). Welner has received the American Educational Research Association's Early Career Award (in 2006) and Palmer O. Johnson Award (best article in 2004), the Rockefeller Foundation's Bellagio Residency, and the post-doctoral fellowship awarded by the National Academy of Education and the Spencer Foundation. Dr. Welner teaches courses in educational policy, program evaluation, school law, and social foundations of education.